Afternoon Tea
at Home
Made Simple

Afternoon Tea at Home
Made simple

Giuliana Orme

Not that I'm angling for an
invitation, but I hope that this
will complement your lifestyle.
Many thanks for your friendship over
the past few years and I do hope
we'll manage to continue our
NT outings.   Yours ever, [Pirate]

Dedication

I would like to dedicate this book to my darling daughter Heloise.

My heartfelt thanks also go to all my students who have been such a source
of inspiration and encouragement.

Acknowledgements

I am extremely grateful to Stephen Twining of the famous tea company, for permission
to use their tea tasting notes and witty descriptions. I am also indebted to Irene Gorman,
Head of the Tea Guild, for her help and guidance; and to William Gorman, Executive
Chairman of the UK Tea Council Ltd and Tea Guild for the information used from their
website (www.tea.co.uk). My thanks also go to Clare Hubbard for her editorial guidance,
Michael Bassett, Nic Laight and Tommy Orme for the food photography and
Edwina Erhman of the Victoria and Albert Museum.

Special thanks to designer Sue Rose, for her creativity, her generosity and her sheer
professionalism and to David Wright and my darling sisters Anita Marovac and
Maria Taylor for their invaluable assistance and encouragement.

And finally… thanks to *all* my friends and loved ones who have given me their
time and support so unstintingly.

Afternoon Tea at Home – *Made Simple*

© 2008 Giuliana Orme

Published by Canonbury Publishing Ltd
Registered Office: Curzon House, 24 High Street, Banstead, Surrey, SM7 2LJ
Registered in England No. 4765425 VAT Reg. Number 811 5700 64

RRP: £14.99 (USA $27)
ISBN: 978-0-9555671-3-1
Printed in the United Kingdom

Contents

INTRODUCTION

IF YOU'RE READING THIS BOOK then we already have something in common – a love and respect for the traditional and a desire to preserve the quintessentially British *Afternoon Tea at Home*. While it is undoubtedly popular (and increasingly so) to enjoy afternoon tea in hotels and tea shops, my quest is to remind everyone that it began, first and foremost, in the home. We need to treasure this lovely, quirky institution and in this book I'm going to do all I can to encourage you to keep the tradition alive and hold a tea party for your friends. And what's more, I'm going to show you exactly how to do it.

So, where does my love of afternoon tea come from? Well, I have always loved baking and cooking – I used to watch my mother prepare delicious food for our big family and as soon as I was old enough I started to bake on my own. I found it so intensely satisfying (and still do!) to mix some fairly basic ingredients together, put them in a tin and then watch them transform and grow in the oven into something as splendid as a cake. The enjoyment didn't end there of course, as I would then serve and enjoy the cake – with lashings of hot tea – with my family and friends.

Around eight years ago, I found myself at a rather difficult time in my life, following the end of my marriage. One of the consequences was that I needed to find a way to support myself financially to enable me to continue living in my beloved family home. I'd taught cooking informally for many years and found it made a wonderful contrast to my work as a relationship counsellor, however, I'd never done it as a profession. The idea came to me – over a cup of tea of course!

I was giving an informal English lesson to a Japanese friend and I noticed how relaxed she was, sitting at my kitchen table having a cup of tea. I initially thought it would be a good idea to combine English conversation lessons with providing afternoon tea but I soon discovered that what people really wanted was to know *how to prepare and serve afternoon tea*. A Japanese friend helped me to word an advert and I offered an afternoon tea course of four lessons at my home, which were very popular. After about a year, I was approached by a Japanese tour company who asked me if I would design a course especially for them to suit visitors to London. This was a real challenge as they wanted me to condense the whole course into one lesson! It took a lot of planning and redesigning, but "where there's a will there's a way", and this is the format that I now offer to all my students. I absolutely love the interaction with my students and visitors and the joy of sharing my home in this way.

This book is another way for me to share my enthusiasm and to teach more people about afternoon tea. The book is divided into two parts: PART 1 shows you how to make, prepare and serve afternoon tea – from boiling the kettle to baking the scones to folding the napkins; PART 2 takes you on a journey from tea plantation to pot, tells the story of the arrival of tea in England, gives you the history of the teapot, explores the health benefits of tea, lists quotations from the "great and the good" and informs you of facts and trivia about tea.

You will see that I'm keen to de-mystify the whole anxiety concerning English etiquette and afternoon tea. My firm belief is that if you are observant and considerate, you will not go far wrong. There are a few little pointers that I can give you, but what I think matters most, is a positive attitude and good old-fashioned kindness.

During my years of teaching I have become aware of a tendency in my students to "get it right" by conforming. I believe very strongly that difference can be something to be celebrated and that "different"

doesn't equal "wrong". I have discovered that making the shortbread with my students is an excellent way of demonstrating this. Because of our individual differences (body temperature, hand pressure etc.) we all take different amounts of time to make the shortbread and I explain that this is neither good nor bad but merely different and that the end results will be equally good. Too much concern to conform can sap creativity and enjoyment.

What I want to do is to encourage you to have the confidence to have a tea party in your own home. I want you to appreciate that putting the stamp of your own individual personality on the occasion and how you present it, will make it extra special and enjoyable for your guests.

I very much hope that the combination of the recipes, the tips that accompany them and all of the suggestions will inspire you to enjoy hosting afternoon tea and to sit with your friends and families to enjoy delicious food and good conversation.

Just remember those lovely wise words, "Food made without love feeds only half the man".

Enjoy!

Giuliana

HOW TO USE THIS BOOK!

We all have our preferred measures and ways of doing things. I've created the recipes throughout this book in grams. If you would prefer to use pounds and ounces the rule is 1 ounce = approximately 28 grams. I found a great free website www.onlineconversion.com which does all the work for you. Just type in the gram amount and it'll convert it into the correct ounces for you!

In this addition I have also included American cups (240ml) due to popular request. For best results, it is important not to mix and match the measures but to stay with either American cups, grams or ounces.

Measuring carefully can make all the difference.

Unlike cooking, baking is more of an exact science so getting the measurements right will make a big difference to the end results. For this reason I like to use digital scales with the gram/kilo system.

1 American cup = 240 ml

Spoon Measurements
1 teaspoon = 5ml
1 tablespoon = 15ml

A Word about Fan Oven Temperatures

When it comes to fan ovens and fan assisted ovens, I strongly advise you to follow your manufacturer's instructions. Some modern fan ovens suggest that the temperature should be 20 degrees lower than the conventional, while fan assisted ovens are normally set at 10 degrees lower. I have found that my new fan oven needs to be 15 degrees lower than the conventional.

PART 1

Serving Afternoon Tea at Home

CHAPTER 1

Style and Presentation of Afternoon Tea

A S A DIRECT RESULT of its Victorian parlour origins, distinguishing features of the afternoon tea ritual are graciousness, elegance and that really old-fashioned word – daintiness! It offers the opportunity to use and share your prettiest china and table linen and enjoy them to the full. Preparing your tea table offers a chance to really indulge your imagination and artistry and express your own personal taste.

TEA TABLE

Afternoon tea is traditionally served in the sitting room with guests seated on easy chairs or sofas around a low table. Actually, the perfect tea table is a coffee table! Make sure that you have enough chairs for your guests and that the table is large enough for all of the food to be laid out on it. Also, try to ensure that there is somewhere for people to put their cups and saucers down. If you have other small tables or stools that you can put next to people's chairs, these are useful for guests to place their cups of tea. Depending on the set-up that you have, the table may also need to be big enough for the tea tray as well (see page 15).

TABLE LINEN AND NAPKINS

A pretty, lacy tablecloth can transform a very ordinary coffee table that is being set for tea. You may have one that belonged to your grandmother or mother. It is lovely to use items with a history and they're a wonderful talking point too, as someone is bound to ask you how you came by it.

While it is nice to use old-fashioned linen napkins they are quite hard work to launder. I have found that there are some exquisite and delicate tea-sized paper napkins, which are an excellent substitute. They come in such a variety of colours and designs and are a thing of beauty in their own right. They tend to be sold in stationers and gift shops and are worth looking out for as you travel around. Some of the loveliest examples are made in Japan. They tend to be of a very delicate structure and are among the favourites in my collection.

FLOWERS

A delicate flower arrangement is always a welcome addition to the tea table. It's best to keep the arrangement low, as flowers that are too tall can upset the aesthetic balance and also block the view of your guests across the table. Here is another opportunity to be creative and inventive. I have recently discovered that a pretty china cup and saucer make a lovely "vase" for delicate flowers. In order to make the flowers secure, you will need to place a stem holder inside the cup. Similarly a charming old teapot makes a lovely centrepiece and is a good way of using an old favourite that is cracked or chipped. Any damaged bits that you don't want to be seen can easily be obscured by the flowers or foliage! Fresias are lovely flowers and are generally available all-year-round, otherwise use whatever blooms are seasonal and suitably delicate.

TEA-SET

Don't think for a minute that holding an afternoon tea party means that you have to have everything matching! There is absolutely no reason why even the teacups and saucers should all be the same (see picture on facing page). For example, I have lots of different cups and saucers decorated with various gold designs and they look very attractive when grouped together on the tea tray. I also have a collection of various flowered teacups and saucers which look very charming. I really think that this originality adds a little extra something to the occasion and gives an added dimension to the general conversation.

Just use your imagination and be innovative. It can be fun to collect individual cups, saucers and plates and you will probably get the "bug" and find yourself searching for new finds when you're out and about. It is worth remembering that if you are gathering together your own collection of individual cups and saucers, it's a good idea to follow a theme such as choosing patterns with flower designs or complementary colours. As long as you like them, then you will serve them with pride and pleasure and that's what will make you and your guests feel good. Expense really doesn't have to be an issue – I have often found

Flowers make the tea table attractive and welcoming.

Just a few of my favourite bits of assorted tea china from my collection.

really charming items for sale in charity shops at very little cost. Whether your finds are from exclusive antique shops or local charity shops is irrelevant. The main point is to find your own style and have fun with it. In fact, I have got so carried away lately that I have now accumulated more than I need and am happy to pass on my bargains to my students, who enjoy buying them as souvenirs!

Setting the Tea Tray

The tea tray is used to carry the items from the kitchen to the room in which you are serving tea. I've listed below the items that you'll need to put on your tea tray. You can use whatever sort of tray you like, but it does need to be sturdy and large enough to hold all of the necessary items. I like to place my tea tray on a separate, higher table away from the tea table, and place the teapot and hot-water jug next to it. This way you have more room on the tea table and also it means that all of the hot liquids are placed safely away from your guests, particularly children. Tea trolleys are great but are best kept for plates and serving food, as you don't want the worry of spilling tea, milk etc.

Here's what you will need to put on your tea tray:

- **Tray cloth** – cover the tray with a pretty cloth, the prettier the better! Aside from looking charming, it does have a practical function – it stops the items on the tray from slipping. If you haven't got a tray cloth to hand, you could use a pretty tea towel or cut a piece of material to fit your tray.

- **Teacups and saucers** – lay out the cups and saucers and have some teaspoons ready for those who like sugar (such people are getting quite rare these days!). This is a good opportunity to use those souvenir spoons that most families seem to have hanging around!

- **Sugar bowl** – with attractive sugar spoon or tongs.

- **Milk jug** – choose a jug that is large enough to hold a reasonable amount of milk for the number of guests that you are serving, otherwise you will have to keep running out to the kitchen to fill it up.

- **Slop bowl** – rest the bowl on a saucer or plate to avoid splashes (see page 17 for more information).

- **Tea strainer** – see page 17.

SERVING PLATES

You can find all sorts of different shaped plates and small trays or dishes for serving sandwiches, cakes and biscuits. In fact, any originality will be an added bonus, because your guests will be fascinated to hear the stories connected to your finds. Cake stands are of course popular, but by no means essential. There are many lovely designs available, both old fashioned and modern.

CUTLERY

Small tea knives and forks add to the gracious, old-fashioned effect, however, any cutlery will do the job, just use what you've got. The knives are used mostly for spreading cream and jam on to scones and the forks are used for eating the cakes. I tend to place the cutlery in a small container in the centre of the table from which people can help themselves as and when they need them. Otherwise they get in the way if you have to balance them on your plate while tucking into your sandwiches!

TEA PLATES

As well as providing small tea plates for the sandwiches, scones and cakes, have some extra plates handy for anyone who wishes to use a fresh plate.

TEA STRAINERS

Unless you are using an infuser teapot (see page 119), you'll need a tea strainer to catch the leaves as the tea is poured into the cups. They usually come with a little bowl to rest the strainer on and catch any drips. Tea strainers are made from various materials and are available in different shapes and styles – from a simple bamboo strainer, to a decorated

---

Using a Tea Strainer

Place strainer over the teacup and pour the tea (slowly) through it. Rest the strainer in its bowl. Pouring the tea slowly through the strainer adds to the general graciousness of the occasion, but it does mean exercising a little patience, a virtue I am sometimes a little short of!

---

porcelain strainer to match your tea service, to an elegant and elaborate sterling silver strainer. Silver tea strainers that sit in a little drip-catching bowl are, of course, very beautiful little objects to own, but you can get perfectly good modern substitutes that do the job effectively.

SLOP BOWLS

This is a highly practical item, used for getting rid of leftover, unwanted tea and dregs from teacups, before pouring in fresh tea. Slop bowls look rather like large sugar bowls. They can be as elegant or as functional as you wish – but preferably not transparent for obvious reasons!

HOT-WATER JUGS

One thing you can't have too much of when serving tea is hot water – you will need lashings of it. To save too much running around once my guests have arrived, I like to fill a large thermal jug (don't forget to pre-warm it) with boiling water just before they are due.

As with teapots, the best value jugs can be found in hardware shops, although I recently spied quite an elegant one in John Lewis, the department store in Oxford Street, London, and the price was very reasonable. If, for whatever reason, you find yourself hosting an afternoon tea party without a hot-water jug, make sure that your kettle is always full and reasonably (and of course safely) accessible.

People usually have very strong personal preferences about how they like their tea – weak or strong. What matters is that you respect the individual tastes and requirements of your guests and serve their tea accordingly. Having the jug of hot water handy makes this quite a simple process.

TEA COSIES

This seems a good point at which to discuss a much joked about and rather old-fashioned teatime accessory, with which I have to admit to having a rather love-hate relationship! There's certainly nothing like an old-fashioned, homemade tea cosy to make you feel somewhat nostalgic for the "good old days"! If you don't have an auntie or granny who is partial to knitting or sewing, fear not – you can certainly buy modern ones. However, if you have taken the trouble to set a pretty tea tray, take care not to ruin it all by using a tea cosy that looks more like an unattractive woolly hat! There are many pretty examples around and some of the nicest are those that have been made by hand. The main thing is that tea cosies are a wonderful way of keeping your precious brew warm. If you can't find a nice tea cosy, place a small patterned fabric napkin or towel over the spout and lid to help retain some of the heat of the pot.

TEAPOTS

Finally, we come to the most important item of all, the teapot. I don't usually place my teapot on the tea tray as it makes it too heavy to carry! I usually put it on a tea stand (anything heatproof will do) and place it near the tea tray.

I seem to have, quite unintentionally, developed quite a collection of teapots over the years, including some miniature ones, which are a great favourite with visiting children. There is a particular little neighbour of mine who has been coming to have tea with me since she was three-years-old. She loves to have all the pretty little cups, milk jug and sugar bowl set out on a tray. Her current favourite is peach tea and she just loves the chance to sit like a little "lady" and play grown-ups. In this case (rather than having extra hot water) I usually have a small jug of cold water handy. She enjoys being allowed to pour it into her cup to cool down her tea. She is particularly partial to the sugar bowl and is very good at distracting me so that she can pop yet another lump of sugar into her mouth, when she thinks I'm not looking!

CHOOSING AND BUYING A TEAPOT

There are almost as many different theories as to what sort of teapot to use, as there are varieties of tea! They are made from many different materials and come in all shapes, sizes, colours and designs. However, as well as considering the style of your teapot, there are a few practical considerations to think about as well.

☕   I think it's important to think about whether you are buying your teapot primarily for practical use or if you would like it to be a work of art and a future investment! Obviously expense is a factor to take into account. It's useful to know that both stainless steel and earthenware teapots are less expensive if purchased in hardware shops as opposed to department stores.

- ☕ Regardless of whether your teapot is intended for everyday use in the kitchen or for elegant tea parties, I think it is very important to choose something that is pleasing to the eye.

- ☕ Teapots made from terracotta or non-rust metals, such as tin and silver, and Yixing teapots (see page 118) gradually develop a tannin "lining" that retains the flavour of the tea. If you are using these types of teapots it is generally recommended to pre-pare just one variety of tea per pot to avoid flavour contamination.

- ☕ If you like to drink different types of tea, it's a good idea to have a pot for black tea, one for smoked tea, a third pot for green tea and one for flavoured tea.

- ☕ Think about the size of teapot and work out, on average, how many cups you would need it to serve.

- ☕ The lid should fit snugly – there is nothing worse than having the lid fall off when you are in the middle of pouring your tea!

- ☕ Check that it pours well. If possible, fill the pot to about three-quarters full with water and test it out to see if it flows without spilling or dribbling.

- ☕ When full, the pot should feel well-balanced in your hand as you lift it.

MY CURRENT FAVOURITE TEAPOTS

The three teapots that I use the most are:

- ☕ Large stainless steel pot (8–10 cups)
- ☕ "Brown Betty" – a traditional, highly-glazed earthen-ware teapot, see illustration left.
- ☕ Bodum® glass infuser* teapot

How to Clean and Care for Your Teapot

Needless to say, opinions differ on the subject of cleaning teapots, in fact some people feel that putting anything, let alone washing-up liquid, anywhere near the inside of a teapot is to be avoided at all costs. However, you do need to take care of your teapot to get the best results from your tea. Here's how to do it:

After using glass, silver, china, porcelain, or glazed earthenware teapots, pour out any remaining tea, rinse with clean water and turn upside-down to drain. Even if you rinse your pots after every use, which is advisable, they will eventually build up stains. To remove the tannin build-up, fill the teapot with a solution of 2 tablespoons of bicarbonate of soda (baking soda) and boiling water, and soak overnight. In the morning, empty the teapot, rinse it thoroughly and let it dry. If you can't be bothered with this, just put some bicarbonate of soda (baking soda) on a soft, wet kitchen brush and give it a good scrub. Again, rinse it thoroughly and allow to dry.

Unglazed teapots – some people consider that the staining on the inside of the pot adds to the flavour, rather similar to seasoning a wok. This thinking applies particularly to unglazed equipment such as Yixing-style pots. In fact, if you are using an unglazed teapot like this, it is generally thought better never to wash or clean the inside at all. Ideally, this type of teapot should only be used for one particular tea, as the lining it acquires from repeated use is important to the flavour of the brewed tea (see page 118).

On special occasions I also use a couple of rather pretty bone china teapots, for no other reason than because they are so pretty!

* The Bodum® pot that I use is a glass infuser teapot. It has an incorporated basket to hold the tea-leaves and a plunger device that prevents the tea from infusing further, once it has been pressed down. I find this pot particularly practical for making perfumed or flavoured teas such as Earl Grey, because the glass does not retain the fragrance of the tea. They produce many different styles of this type of pot. Just choose the one you like the look of.

CHAPTER 2

Making and Serving a Really Good Pot of Tea

WHILE THE TASTY SANDWICHES, tempting scones and delicious cakes may make your guests "ooh" and "aah", the real star of the afternoon tea is the tea itself. There is so much to say about tea, it is really a subject for a book all of its own and many wonderful books have been written on it. If you really become enthused about the subject, there is a lot to learn. But, if you just want to know enough to serve a good pot of tea at your afternoon tea party, everything you need to know is right here. On pages 84–96 I have devoted a chapter to tea varieties and their characteristics. Go to these pages to help you decide what tea variety to choose. In this chapter I'm going tell you about my tried and tested options, give you a few buying and storage tips, and then take you step-by-step through the process of making the perfect "cuppa".

WHAT TEA TO CHOOSE

If you are following the fine traditions and history of afternoon tea, then there is really no substitute for the real thing – namely, leaf tea. Having said this, there are some really good brands of tea bag around and many of them are now becoming available in individual tea varieties as well as blends. Not that I'm criticising blends, some of them can be really successful – so be confident, follow your nose and choose what you like and can afford.

People often ask me which brands of tea I prefer. The truth is that (as with clothes) I am not overly concerned about labels! Luckily for us, today's tea production standards are pretty high and most major brands take great care to produce very good quality tea. However, when possible, I prefer to buy organic, just as I do with other foods.

MY CURRENT FAVOURITE TEAS

Here are my favourites in alphabetical order:

- Assam
- Ceylon
- Darjeeling
- Earl Grey
- Fortnum and Mason's Royal Blend

STORING TEA

To gain the maximum flavour from your tea, whether leaf tea or tea bags, it is important to store it properly. When choosing containers for storing tea, it helps to remember that tea is sensitive to light, moisture and odours from strong-smelling foods and spices. So it should be stored in a cool, dry place, in containers that are opaque and airtight. This means, of course, that those pretty glass storage jars that people often like to use are not suitable as they expose the tea to light.

Two Teas Please

I find that guests welcome the opportunity of tasting different teas and I usually serve at least two varieties, one after the other, rather than making two pots at the same time. I do it this way because it makes it easier to manage and anything that makes the hostess more relaxed is ultimately good for the guests!

It's important to remember that all tea has a shelf life. If stored properly, good black tea will keep for at least a year. Green and white tea, however, should definitely be consumed in less than a year and oolong would typically fall somewhere in between. Check the "best before" dates on packets. In fact, it is the issue of freshness that is of utmost importance to successful tea-making. Better to have a fresh packet of supermarket brand tea, than an out-of-date version of something from a more exclusive retailer. Taste is the best judge of freshness. You can easily tell if your tea is past its best, as it will have lost its aroma and will make either a bitter or dull-tasting cup.

BREWING TEA

Before I start to explain the secrets of perfectly-brewed tea, in order to avoid any confusion I would like to point out that the words "infusing", "steeping" and "brewing" are all interchangeable!

Even the very finest tea, chosen with great care and precision, can be a great disappointment if it isn't properly brewed. With correct steeping, the natural acids present give maximum flavour to the tea, but when oversteeped or overbrewed, it is these same agents that cause bitterness. These natural acids were formerly called "tannins" but are now referred to as "polyphenols" (see page 124).

To make a stronger tea, it is generally better to increase the amount used rather than to lengthen the brewing time. It's also important to recognise that strength of tea cannot be judged by colour – some teas brew to a light shade (e.g. Earl Grey) while others (like Yorkshire tea) make a dark liquid.

On average, tea is steeped for three to five minutes depending on the type of tea and personal taste. The most important variables to take into account are the size of the leaf and the temperature of the water. Generally, the larger the leaf, the longer you must steep it; the smaller the leaf, the more surface it exposes to the water and the more quickly infusion occurs.

Fruit and Herbal Tisanes

Fruit and herbal tisanes may be steeped for as long as you like without causing bitterness, as they don't have the same constituents as real tea (see page 50).

Let's look at some examples:

- **Small leaves,** such as English and Irish Breakfast blends and Assam teas, generally steep for three minutes.
- **Medium leaves,** like Ceylon and Orange Pekoe (a basic medium grade black tea) are best when brewed for four to five minutes.
- **Large leaves,** such as Oolong, Jasmine and Earl Grey, should brew for five to six minutes.

A STEP-BY-STEP GUIDE TO MAKING THE PERFECT POT OF TEA

Remember that part of the enjoyment and relaxation that tea provides, comes from taking the time necessary to prepare it properly. In fact, the ritual of making tea can be very soothing in itself.

You will need:
Leaf tea or tea bags (black tea)
Suitable teapot
Tea kettle
Timer
Hot-water jug (preferably thermal)

1. Fill an empty kettle with freshly-drawn (or filtered) cold water.

☕ The freshness of the water is important, as fresh water contains more oxygen, which enhances the taste of the tea. Running the tap a little before filling the kettle allows the water to become fully aerated (oxygenated). Unless you are seriously worried about the quality of your water there is no need to use bottled water.

Brewing with Bags
When using tea bags, it is best to squeeze them gently before removing. In general, tea bags should be steeped for less time than leaf tea because they are comprised of finely-chopped tea, which brews faster.

2. Before the water boils, pour some into the teapot and swirl it around to warm the pot before emptying it.

☕   As well as keeping the tea hot for longer, a warmed teapot helps to maintain the water temperature during the steeping process, allowing for better and more complete extraction of flavour.

3. Place the tea or tea bags into the heated pot and make sure that the teapot is close to the kettle.

☕   Ideally you need about 1 rounded teaspoon of dry leaves for each 175-millilitre (6 fluid-ounce) cup. The general rule is to use 1 teaspoon of tea (or one tea bag) per person and "one for the pot"! This amount will vary according to the type of tea and personal taste. In practice I have found that this can produce very strong tea indeed. I like to use 6 teaspoons of tea in my large (8–10 cups) teapot and 4 teaspoons in the pot for 6 cups.

4. Immediately the water boils, pour it directly onto the tea, give it a brisk stir and put the lid on the pot. Don't overfill the pot, as it will make it difficult to pour and could be dangerous.

☕   "Take the pot to the kettle not the kettle to the pot", is the standard rule when making tea. The water should be at a full rolling boil when poured on to the tea leaves to release the full flavour. Underboiled water will result in a weak tea, while overboiled or reboiled water loses the oxygen required to bring out the full flavour, and even the finest tea will taste flat.

5. Allow to brew before pouring, as mentioned previously, this is generally between 3–5 minutes, according to the type of tea.

☕   If using an infuser, lift it out of the teapot as soon as the tea has finished steeping (unless it has the type of infuser with a plunger which, when pressed down, separates the leaves from the infused tea).

For actual amounts of tea, water temperatures and brewing times, it is advisable to follow the recommendations given on the package for the particular tea you are making. As I mentioned earlier – generally, the larger the leaf, the longer it takes to infuse. With experience you can experiment with the steeping time according to your own personal taste (i.e. do you prefer strong tea or weak tea?). But remember that oversteeping tea will cause bitterness.

If you are not using a teapot with an integral infuser and you are concerned about over-infusing your tea, then once you have poured out the tea for your guests, you can strain the remainder into another (warmed) pot. I personally don't do this as it's quite fussy. After having poured the first few cups, I often top up the teapot with extra hot water (from my thermal jug) and this "freshens" the brew.

CHAPTER 3

Etiquette and Form

Harmony, respect, purity and tranquility – these are the principles of Chanoyu (the Japanese tea ceremony), handed down by the tea master Sen-no Rikyu, which tea practitioners endeavour to integrate into their daily lives. What a beautiful and inspirational legacy to leave to the world. While it is undeniably the case that the English afternoon tea is a much simpler ritual, I would like to think that these same principles are relevant.

When you take into consideration the fact that the tradition of afternoon tea stems from the Victorian era, it is not surprising that there are still some rather outdated and essentially snobbish notions that have attached themselves to this lovely ritual. A traditional Victorian afternoon tea party was performed according to certain rules of etiquette, but it is very important to remember that, as in all aspects of life, we have to move with the times and adapt accordingly!

I am a great believer in courtesy and kindness. I would not, for one moment, like to give the impression that I wish to recommend a lowering of standards when it comes to etiquette and manners; quite the opposite, in fact. What I am talking about here is my dislike of a slavish mentality to etiquette and form for its own sake. This puts so-called "correctness" over consideration of people and their feelings. So it is with this thought firmly in mind that I will discuss the much asked question…

MILK FIRST OR MILK AFTERWARDS?

There seems to be an awful lot of "hoo-ha" about the whole business of whether the milk, if taken, should be added to the cup before or after pouring the tea. It is known as the "milk in first" (M.I.F.) debate. This is a classic example of the sort of issue that is often associated with snobbery and is fussed about by people who believe there is only one "right" way to do things. Let me state from the outset that my feeling is that (in this instance) you should do whatever you are most comfortable with. Like most things in life, there are pros and cons for both options!

The Origins of M.I.F. Snobbery

Historically, it was pure practicality that gave rise to the idea of pouring milk into the cup first in order to prevent the hot tea from cracking the cup. However, the superior bone china used by the wealthy was able to withstand the effects of very hot tea. By pouring the tea into the cup first, people were, in effect, advertising the fact that they could afford expensive china that could withstand very hot temperatures. The snobbishness that has grown around this whole issue is largely due to this fact.

However, I am glad to say that in recent times, scientific experimentation has laid the subject open to question and debate. Scientists have focused on how adding the milk afterwards affects the flavour. Some claim that adding the milk to the larger mass of hot tea scalds the milk. You won't be surprised to hear that others have decided quite the opposite! So it is entirely up to you.

Some Helpful Tips

If you put the milk in first and then pour in the hot tea, it has the effect of mixing the tea so that you can judge (from the colour) by the time you have poured half a cup, if the strength of the tea is going to be satisfactory. If it is too weak, then you can wait for the tea to infuse a little longer before continuing to fill the cup. If it's really much too weak, it's best to empty it out and start again, using less milk the next time!

If you pour the tea into the cup first, then once you have added the milk, you will need to give it a little stir in order to properly see the finished result and adjust it as necessary by adding more milk or hot water. It is also worth mentioning that tea poured directly into the cup causes much more staining than it does if the milk is added first. Something to think about if you're going to be doing the washing-up!

I grew up (in the north of England) using the "milk in first" method and so am probably pretty good at judging the correct amount of milk needed – it's just a matter of what suits you best. I have found that a foolproof way to please your guests is to give them a choice. I ask "would you like your milk poured first or afterwards?" This way everyone is happy.

One last thing to mention – some people don't like milk in their tea at all! Some people drink it black and others like it served with a slice of fresh lemon.

The Royal Way

Incidentally, just for the record, you might be interested to know that Queen Elizabeth II prefers to pour her milk in afterwards. She clearly doesn't have to worry too much about washing up her cups! Apparently Earl Grey is one of her favourite varieties of tea.

Milk Q&A

Q *What kind of milk is best to serve with tea?*
A Some people insist on full cream milk for authenticity and traditionalists believe that it brings out the best flavour in the tea, but I find that I also enjoy the flavour of semi-skimmed milk.

Q *Are all teas served with milk?*
A This is partly down to personal taste, however, it is generally accepted that green tea is not suited to the addition of milk. Generally speaking, strong black teas, such as Assam, Kenyan etc., are particularly well-suited to the addition of milk.

Q *Can you serve cream with tea?*
A The answer is a definite "No!" Confusion over this probably derives from a difference in the terms used for milk and cream in the UK and USA. When an American host or hostess asks if you would like "cream" in your tea, the "cream" referred to is actually milk or a milk substitute. This is not always the case when serving coffee, when cream is a very deli-

cious option. Here's a sobering thought: Tibetan people are reputed to enjoy their tea flavoured with rancid yak butter!

Q *Should the milk be heated?*
A No. Cold milk is always served with tea. Heating the milk alters the flavour.

How Much Milk?

A really good pot of well-infused tea can be adjusted to the individual taste of your guests by the addition, according to preference, of either extra milk or extra hot water to each cup. Some people like to have really strong tea made "weak" with lots of milk. Other people prefer to have their tea "weakened" with water and served with less milk.

SUGAR

The issue here is whether to use sugar lumps or ground sugar. If you happen to have some sugar tongs and can obtain sugar lumps easily, then go for it! But don't feel that you have to use sugar lumps. Use them if you want to. Otherwise, there is absolutely nothing wrong with using ground granulated or caster sugar. I would certainly advise serving white sugar as opposed to brown (because of the flavour) but other than that, it couldn't matter less. Incidentally, I've noticed that very few people seem to take sugar these days anyway!

POURING THE TEA

Historically, at intimate gatherings, the hostess herself would pour the tea, while seated with her guests. (At a large gathering, it was perfectly acceptable for the hostess to ask a couple of personal friends to help her with the pouring.) Guests were asked, "Do you take sugar? One lump or two?" and the sugar was placed in the cup using sugar tongs. Then she would ask, "Milk, or lemon?" For the lemon-takers, a plate garnished with thinly sliced lemon was offered with a small fork. After handing the cup to the guest, hot water

I'll Be Mother

It's usual that when a group of friends sit down to take tea in a teashop or hotel, one of the group will volunteer to pour by saying "I'll be mother". Funnily enough, men say this too, although, of course, it is said slightly tongue in cheek! The origins of this phrase date back to a time when tea was so expensive that it was kept under lock and key in a tea caddy and only opened by "mother" or the lady of the household who was in charge of the key!

was offered for those who liked a weaker infusion.

I don't have any issues with this traditional approach unless the arrangement of the furniture or the presence of small children makes it more appropriate for the tea to be poured from a higher side-table or sideboard. This may require the pourer to be standing up, but the tea will taste just as good and there will be less danger of anyone accidentally knocking over pots of hot tea and hot-water jugs!

The important thing to remember when holding an afternoon tea party is that while it is nice to observe traditions and etiquette, the important thing is that you and your guests enjoy the experience. So never be frightened to enlist one or two friends to help you pour the tea. If you try to do it all yourself, you will be up and down like a jack-in-the-box and exhausted to boot! If you are comfortable about doing so, it is also perfectly acceptable to encourage guests to help themselves after the first cup. This makes for a very friendly and relaxed atmosphere and that's, after all, what you want to encourage.

SERVING AND EATING SCONES

When serving scones, you will need to provide small dessert knives (see page 16). The knives are used to cut the scones in half and for spreading the jam and cream on to the scones.

When you are eating the scones, it is equally correct to first cut the scone in half horizontally, or to gently twist and pull it in half with your fingers.

Which goes first, the jam or the cream? This is one of those issues that people tend to get unnecessarily fussed about. Once you have a scone on your plate, just help yourself to a spoonful of jam and cream and place them towards the outer edge of the plate, rather than directly onto the scone. It really doesn't matter which is spread first – just do what you are most comfortable with. I tend to think of the thick cream as a sort of butter substitute and so I spread that on the halved scone first and then top it with some jam.

Incidentally, I always like to have a box of tissues handy as well as providing napkins, because eating jam and cream can be a messy business!

SERVING AND EATING CAKE

When serving cake for afternoon tea, it is always helpful to provide small dessert forks. There are little cake forks made especially for the purpose and they can be very attractive. However, any small forks will do (see page 16). You can place the cakes whole on the tea table or cut them into slices in the kitchen and arrange them on a serving plate.

When eating cake, instead of using a dessert fork, some people prefer to cut small pieces of cake with their knife and then pick up the pieces by hand. Either method is "correct", so choose whichever way feels more natural to you. I always think that good manners are essentially about kindness and consideration. So, as long as the way in which you are eating isn't in any way unsightly or off-putting to others, you're probably getting it right. It's also really important that you feel relaxed and comfortable, because those feelings will be picked up by those around you.

CONVERSATION TIME

Afternoon tea presents a golden opportunity for conversation to flow – just like the tea! You won't be surprised to know that a large part of the conversation that diverted the Victorian ladies centred around gossip!

Even short periods of silence between conversation can make some people a little anxious, so it is always good to have some soft music playing in the background. Of course, silences may well occur because your guests are busy tucking into your delicious spread!

Music

Music not only adds to the general pleasure and relaxation of the event but it can also be a talking point in itself. Take a little time before your guests arrive to sort out some suitable music that you particularly like. It is generally advisable to choose something reasonably melodic and soothing. Beware of giving your guests indigestion by playing fast, rhythmic music, which tends to increase the pace at which people eat!

My "Conversation Box"

One of my great pleasures is serving afternoon tea to overseas students and friends who are often experiencing afternoon tea in an English home for the first time. Bearing in mind that for many of them English is not their first language, I have tried to come up with ways of helping the conversation to flow. Often, in my efforts to encourage people to chat, I am aware that I'm asking rather a lot of questions! Of course, the last thing I want is for people to feel they are being interrogated, so in order to make this a more shared and fun process, I have developed what I call my "conversation box".

Using some thin, coloured card, cut out some simple flower shapes. Write some questions on the back (see opposite). Put the questions in a really pretty box – the kind that you don't mind leaving around! Mine is from one of those perfume gift sets but a pretty chocolate box or biscuit tin would serve equally well. Or you could be creative and make something funky!

Fascinating Tea Facts and Quotes

Another lovely ice-breaker is to gather a collection of famous quotations and fascinating facts on the subject of tea and encourage your guests to "dip" into them and read them out, if they wish. Consequently, I have had a lot of fun collecting these sayings and quirky bits of information and would love to share them with you (see pages 128–141).

CONVERSATION BOX

Here are just a few examples of the questions in my conversation box. I'm sure you will have fun thinking up your own on a wide variety of subjects.

TRAVEL Which country would you most like to visit next and why?

COLOUR How important is colour to you?

FILMS/SHOWS/THEATRE What film or show have you seen lately? What film would you most like to see?

MUSIC What was the last piece of music you bought?

FLOWERS What is your favourite flower and why?

SPORT What sport do you most enjoy - in terms of either watching or playing?

SOUVENIRS What would you choose to take as souvenirs to friends or relations living overseas?

FOOD What is your favourite dessert?

ENGLAND What would you say is the most enjoyable aspect of living/staying in England?

NAMES If you had to change your first name, what would you choose instead?

FOOD If you could choose any nationality of cuisine for a special meal out - which would it be?

CHAPTER 4

How to Prepare a Really Delicious Afternoon Tea

HERE IS MY FAVOURITE "tried and tested" afternoon tea menu. The quantities given for the sandwiches and the scones are suitable for six people if they are served with all the other items on the menu. You'll probably find there will be plenty of leftovers if you serve the cake, shortbread, Florentines and teabread. Any remaining cake is best popped in the freezer, while all the other items will store very well in airtight containers in the fridge.

Giuliana's Afternoon Tea Menu

Smoked salmon pinwheel sandwiches on brown bread

Egg mayonnaise sandwiches on brown bread

Cucumber sandwiches on white bread

Warm Devonshire scones served with clotted cream and strawberry conserve

Traditional Victoria sandwich cake

Scottish shortbread (petticoat tails)

Teabread – Banana bread, or
Spicy date, apricot and nut loaf

Florentines

Choice of teas: Earl Grey, Darjeeling, Ceylon, Assam
and Fortnum and Mason Royal Blend
– served with milk or lemon slices

AFTERNOON TEA SANDWICHES *(see picture on page 43)*

Well-cut little sandwiches with delicious fillings are a delight. I like to arrange all of the sandwiches on one platter, but this is very much a matter of personal preference. You may like to put each type of sandwich on a separate plate. Before I explain how to make the sandwiches, I'm going to share with you my tips on the essentials of bread and butter and the equipment that you'll need.

Bread

Make sure that you buy good-quality sliced bread. Not many places sell thinly sliced bread these days and even when they do, it doesn't tend to be of the best quality. I usually buy the thinnest of the medium sliced bread. Judge for yourself, because different varieties vary in thickness.

Butter

It is really important to have your butter at the right temperature so that it is easy to spread. If the butter is too cold it will simply rip your bread. Putting cold, hard butter in the microwave for a few seconds on the defrost setting can make all the difference. But watch out because you don't want to end up with a nasty yellow puddle! I find that it's best to do it in bursts of about 10 seconds until it's just the right consistency.

Equipment

It can be so disappointing to get underway with preparations for making your sandwiches, only to discover halfway through that you are missing a vital piece of equipment. To try and ensure against this, I have compiled the following checklist that will serve you well.

☕   **Sharp bread knife** – this will make all the difference to the look of your cut sandwiches. If your bread knife isn't too good, take it somewhere to be sharpened. You'll often find that places where they cut keys will offer this service. Otherwise, splash out and buy a really good one – it will pay you dividends in sandwich-making results!

Mandoline (or slicing attachment on a food processor) – an excellent way of getting really thin slices of cucumber. It's always nicer to have layers of thinly sliced cucumber in a sandwich rather than one layer of thick slices.

Spreading knife – the most practical type of knife to use is a small palette knife. Otherwise look through your knives and choose the one that has the roundest and widest blade.

Kitchen paper towel and cling film (Saran Wrap) – there's nothing worse than sandwiches that dry up and start curling at the edges and these two items are invaluable for keeping your sandwiches fresh and moist. I like to use dampened (plain white) kitchen paper towel covered with cling film to keep them in perfect condition until needed. Simply dampen sheets of kitchen paper towel under the cold tap, squeeze out the excess water and then lay them over your prepared sandwiches. Cover with cling film and refrigerate.

Potato masher – I find this such a useful little gadget for chopping up the hard-boiled eggs for egg sandwiches. Failing this, a fork and some patience work equally well!

Afternoon Tea

Cucumber Sandwiches

These are a must for afternoon tea as they epitomise the spirit of the occasion.

4 thin slices of white bread Softened butter	½ cucumber, (peeled if you prefer, but I don't), thinly sliced

1. Cut the crusts off the slices of white bread and spread with softened butter, making sure you spread right up to the edges.

2. Place the slices of cucumber on two slices of the bread. Put the other two slices of bread on top and cut into small squares or oblongs. You may season the cucumber if you wish, but I prefer the freshness of the cucumber to "do the talking" and it contrasts well with other, stronger tasting fillings.

3. Arrange attractively on a plate, using halved slices of cucumber to decorate.

Smoked Salmon Pinwheel Sandwiches

These attractive little "mouthfuls" always make a lovely addition to a tray of sandwiches and are much easier to make than they look! I like to make them with smoked salmon or with thin slices of smoked ham and cream cheese. Apart from the delicious flavours of these fillings, the colour of both the salmon or the ham make a lovely contrast with the bread.

4 thin slices of brown bread	Freshly ground black pepper
Softened butter or cream cheese	English (curly) parsley and thin slices of
150 g (5 oz) thin slices of smoked salmon	lemon to garnish
Fresh lemon juice	

1. Cut the crusts from the bread.

2. Fold pieces of kitchen paper towel in half and then cut them in half. They will now be roughly the same size as the bread slices. Dampen the kitchen paper towel under the cold tap and then squeeze out the excess water. Place the dampened pieces of kitchen towel under the slices of bread. In case you're wondering, the dampened kitchen towel facilitates the rolling of the sandwiches by keeping the bread moist and also helps to prevent the bread from cracking.

3. Spread butter or cream cheese on the bread, making sure you go right to the edges.

Pinwheel Sandwiches

1 Cut the crusts from the bread

2 Place the dampened pieces of kitchen towel under the slices of bread. Place salmon on top, adding lemon juice.

3 Season with pepper.

4 Roll up the bread using the paper to guide you.

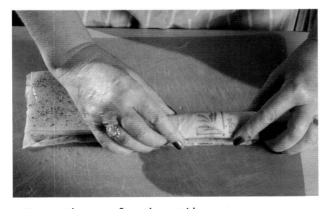

5 Remove the paper from the outside.

6 Slice into pinwheel sandwiches.

tip If your bread is too thick to roll you can always "thin it out" by rolling over it with a rolling pin, before buttering of course!

4. Cover each piece of bread with slices of salmon. Sprinkle lightly with fresh lemon juice and some freshly ground black pepper.

5. Roll up each topped slice of bread as tightly and firmly as possible, using the dampened paper to help you – then discard the paper.

6. Chill for at least 20 minutes or so before cutting each roll into six slices.

7. I like to serve these pinwheel sandwiches in slightly overlapping vertical rows, decorated with English (curly) parsley and thin slices of lemon.

Egg Mayonnaise Sandwiches

2 medium eggs, hardboiled (*see tips*)
Salad cream or mayonnaise (*see tips*)
4 slices of brown bread (I prefer the taste and appearance of brown bread with this egg filling, but use white if you prefer)

Softened butter
Freshly ground black pepper – lots of it!
Salad cress for garnishing

1. Prepare the filling by finely chopping the hardboiled eggs and mixing with enough salad cream or mayonnaise to make a moist, but not wet, filling. Add plenty of freshly ground black pepper.

2. Cut the crusts off the bread and spread with softened butter, making sure you butter right up to the edges. (This is to ensure that the sandwiches stick together well).

3. Spread two buttered slices of bread with a generous amount of the egg filling and top

with the remaining buttered slices.

4. I like to cut these sandwiches into small triangles for variety. Cut each sandwich diagonally, both ways, into four, and then cut each triangle in half again. Or, cut each sandwich into four squares and then cut each square diagonally in half. You should have 16 triangles in total.

5. Sprinkle these tasty sandwiches with a generous amount of salad cress.

tip To hardboil the eggs: cover the eggs with cold water, bring to the boil and simmer gently for 9 minutes. Cool under cold, running water before removing the shells.

tip I like to use salad cream because of the slight sweetness, which goes so well with the egg and the spiciness of the pepper.

Alternative Sandwich Fillings

No doubt you will have lots of ideas of your own for sandwich fillings and you're sure to want to include your own favourites. The following are a few suggestions to remind you of suitable possibilities for teatime:

- **Pâté**
- **Smoked cod's roe**
- **Ham**
- **Crabmeat and mayonnaise**
- **Cold salmon and watercress**
- **Seasoned cream cheese**

A Word About Crusts

Most recipe books tell you to remove the crusts after buttering and filling. I find this incredibly wasteful. I like to remove the crusts before buttering and filling. If you butter right up to the edges and press the sandwiches down firmly before cutting, you will get excellent results and end up with crusts that can be well utilised and not covered with bits of filling. Again, I would like to reiterate that it is important to use a well-sharpened bread knife for best results.

Using Up the Crusts

If you make lots of sandwiches you'll never be short of croutons or breadcrumbs!

Breadcrumbs

These homemade golden breadcrumbs can be used to coat slices of chicken breast or fish fillets etc. The best way to store them is in the freezer. Pop them into a well-sealed food bag or food storage box. Use the breadcrumbs straight from the freezer; this way they will always be fresh.

1. Place the crusts on a baking tray and bake them until golden in colour. The best and most economical way of doing this is to put them in the oven when you are baking something else.

2. Whiz the baked crusts in your food processor until you have fine crumbs. If you don't have a food processor or liquidiser, just put the baked crusts into a bag and crush them with a rolling pin. N.B. This is great therapy if you've got some anger to unleash!

Crust "Croûtons"

These may not be the most elegant-looking croûtons, but they certainly taste good. The best time to prepare these is straight after removing the crusts from the bread. This is because it only takes a few seconds and you may as well while you have the knife and bread board handy, as it's probably not something you will be bothered to do later on. I don't suggest baking these little croûtons in the oven (which I might do with larger cubes) as they are so small they are likely to burn rather easily.

1. Line up several crusts together lengthwise and cut across them to make little "squares". Keep them covered until you are ready to fry them. These store well in the 'fridge.

2. I like to use light and mild olive oil to fry these little croûtons. Heat the oil in a frying pan until it is really hot. Add the bread and fry until golden. A little finely chopped garlic or even a dash of sweet chilli sauce make tasty additions. Lemon-flavoured oil also makes a nice variation.

3. Drain the croûtons well on kitchen paper towel to absorb any excess oil.

SCONES

The secret to a successful afternoon tea lies in the ability to bake and serve really good scones. Delicious, freshly-baked homemade scones are probably the ultimate hallmark of a wonderful afternoon tea. There's nothing like the welcoming smell of homebaking to make friends feel that you've really gone to trouble on their behalf. Paradoxically, there's nothing easier and quicker to make and bake than really good scones! It's simply a question of having the right recipe and methodology. Even if your friends arrive early and "catch you in the act", so to speak, you will gain brownie points for authenticity!

Turn over the page for my special scone recipes.

Scone/Skohn/Skon – Where Did the Term Originate?

This Scottish "quick bread" is said to have taken its name from the Stone of Destiny or Scone, the place where Scottish kings were once crowned. The original triangular-shaped scone was made with oats and cooked on a griddle.

Apart from the classic afternoon tea scones that are served with cream and jam, there are also other types of scone, such as drop scones that are made from a kind of sweet batter and cooked on top of the stove. Drop scones are also known by several other names – Scotch pancakes, girdle cakes and pikelets.

Rich Devonshire Scones

I've tried and tested so many recipes in an attempt to find one that really "delivers the goods" and I hope that you enjoy the results of this one as much as I do. It is essential not to overdo the baking powder as this can result in a rather unpleasant chemical taste. Incidentally, it is because of the addition of the egg that these scones are called "rich". As long as you stick closely to the measurements and the methodology, making and baking the scones is really simple and only takes a matter of minutes from start to finish. The scones are best when served freshly baked, straight from the oven.

MAKES 15 OR 16 SMALL SCONES

300 g (2⅓ cups) plain white flour	Approx. 150 ml (approx ⅔ cup) milk
2½ level teaspoons baking powder	(*see step* 4)
Pinch of salt	60 g (⅓ cup) of soft margarine
1 large egg	(I use sunflower margarine)
	60 g (4 level Tablespoons) white sugar

1. Preheat the oven – conventional 220°C, 425° F, gas mark 7 (hot).

2. Place the flour, baking powder and salt into a medium-sized bowl and stir well. Leave to "sit", while you complete steps 3 and 4. This gives the baking powder time to interact with the flour.

3. Grease a baking tray and dust with flour or line with baking parchment or silicone paper.

4. Crack the egg into a measuring jug and whisk lightly. Add enough milk to make up to approximately 200 ml (¾ cup) of liquid in all and lightly whisk again.

5. Sieve the flour mixture into a large bowl. Add the margarine and rub it in with your

fingertips, until the mixture resembles fine breadcrumbs.

6. Stir in the sugar.

7. Mix in sufficient egg/milk mixture to produce a soft, slightly sticky dough. I find a fork is best for this. You will definitely have some of the egg and milk mixture left over. This can be used to glaze the tops of the scones before baking.

8. Turn the dough on to a floured board and knead very lightly – just enough to remove any cracks. Using your hands, flatten the dough to a thickness of about 2 cm (¾ in). Use a metal pastry cutter to cut the dough into 5-cm (2-in) rounds.

9. Place the dough rounds onto the prepared baking tray so that they are almost touching. This is a little trick I've learnt – it gives the scones soft sides, making them extra moist. Place further apart if you prefer them crusty all over. Brush the tops of the scones with some of the remaining egg and milk mixture and bake for about 9–10 minutes or until golden brown and well-risen.

10. Immediately after removing the scones from the oven, I like to put them straight on to a clean, thick tea towel and wrap them up like "precious babies" to keep them warm (and soft inside) until needed!

The Secrets of Good Scones

☕ The dough mixture should not be too dry – it should feel slightly sticky.

☕ It's best to use a metal pastry cutter for cutting out the scones. If you already have a plastic cutter then you can probably make do with it, but if you're buying a cutter specially, then go for a metal one as they usually do a better job.

tip Don't handle the dough too much – cut out the scones quickly and bake.

STOP PRESS

Just yesterday, while preparing afternoon tea for some guests, I made the scone dough in advance and placed the uncooked rounds in the fridge for 2 hours before baking. They turned out beautifully, so it was a very successful experiment!

Make Your Own "Pastry Brush"

A pastry brush is very useful for glazing the scones before baking. If you don't have one to hand, then do what I do when I can't find mine! Scrunch up a piece of moistened paper kitchen towel and, working quickly, use it as a "brush".

Freezing the Scones

If you really can't make the scones just before your guests arrive (but remember how welcomed they will feel by that magic aroma!) then bake them beforehand, allow to cool and then freeze them immediately.

To serve the scones, take them straight from the freezer and place in a preheated oven – conventional 200°C, 400° F, gas mark 6. They will take about 7–8 minutes to heat up. Do check the timing, as ovens vary so much. If you pop them in the oven when your guests have started to eat their sandwiches, you will probably find that the timing is about right.

Presentation

The presentation of the scones is, of course, quite important. If you don't have a special plate to hand, a small wicker basket can look attractive, or line a bowl with a pretty paper napkin. I was once given a rather lovely piece of table linen from Portugal, designed for serving bread rolls, and it seems to work really well for hot scones (see picture on page 47).

VARIATIONS

While the previous recipe is a classic one, you can make fruit scones or savoury cheese scones using the classic mixture with a few additions.

Fruit scones – add a handful of dried fruit of your choice (sultanas or small raisins work particularly well) to the mixture, before adding the egg and milk.

Savoury cheese scones – English mustard powder, cayenne pepper or paprika and Cheddar cheese are added. To simplify things, I've written it out in full.

Savoury Cheese Scones

These are a special favourite of mine. They are also a wonderful standby for those times when the fridge is a little empty and you want something quick and tasty to eat. I like to serve them with slightly salted, cold English butter. If you're serving them to guests, small squares of butter or butter curls or balls garnished with a sprig of parsley look very appetising when placed alongside.

MAKES 15 SMALL SCONES

300 g (2⅓ cups) plain white flour	1 large egg
2½ level teaspoons baking powder	Approx. 150ml (approx. ⅔ cup) milk
Pinch of salt	(*see step* 4)
1 level teaspoon English mustard powder	60 g (⅓ cup) margarine
Generous pinch of cayenne pepper or	125 g (approx. 1 cup when grated)
paprika	mature Cheddar cheese, coarsely grated

1. Preheat the oven – conventional 220°C, 425°F, gas mark 7 (hot)

2. Place the flour, baking powder, salt, mustard and cayenne pepper into a medium-sized

bowl and stir well. Leave to "sit" while you complete steps 3 and 4. This gives the baking powder time to interact with the flour.

3. Grease a baking tray and dust with flour or line with with baking parchment or silicone paper.

4. Crack the egg into a measuring jug and whisk lightly. Add enough milk to make up approximately 200 ml (approx. ¾ cup) of liquid in all and lightly whisk again.

5. Sieve the flour mixture into a large bowl. Add the margarine and rub it in with your fingertips, until the mixture resembles fine breadcrumbs.

6. Stir in two-thirds of the grated cheese.

7. Stir in sufficient egg/milk mixture to produce a soft, slightly sticky dough. I find a fork is best for this. You will definitely have some of the egg and milk mixture left over. This can be used to glaze the tops of the scones before baking.

8. Turn the dough on to a floured board and knead very lightly – just enough to remove any cracks. Using your hands, flatten the dough to a thickness of about 2 cm (¾ in). Use a plain metal pastry cutter to cut the dough into 5-cm (2in) rounds.

9. Place the dough rounds onto the prepared baking tray. Brush the tops of the scones with some of the remaining egg/milk mixture and sprinkle the rest of the grated cheese evenly over the top. Bake for about 10 minutes or until golden brown and well-risen.

The Cream to Serve with Devonshire Scones

If you're going to be truly authentic about your traditional English afternoon tea, then clotted cream is what the Scots would call the "real McCoy". It is very rich and calorie-laden, with a minimum fat content of 55 per cent, but it is also very delicious! If you are not familiar with using it, when you first open the container it can look a bit odd. It has a yellow layer of clots or coagulated clumps of cream on the top. I certainly haven't made that sound very appealing – have I?! No harm in giving it a little stir to distribute the lumps more evenly.

Clotted cream is traditionally made in Devon and Cornwall (in the south west of England) by separating the cream from the milk and slowly "scalding" it until it is extra thick. As this is not something that is easily made at home, fortunately it is usually available from large supermarkets or speciality stores. If you can't get hold of it, whipped double cream is an excellent alternative.

Traditional Clotted Cream Recipe

I thought you might be interested to hear how it was traditionally made, so here is a lovely old-fashioned recipe. **Need I add that I don't for one minute recommend that you try it!**

"Take 2 gallons of milk straight from the cow, preferably a high butterfat milk producer such as Jersey or Guernsey. Leave to stand undisturbed overnight in a large, wide metal pan, giving the cream a chance to rise to the top. The following morning heat slowly, (scald being the proper term) but do not let boil for about an hour. During this time undulations will form on the surface – a semi-firm thick, slightly yellow crust of cream.

Take off the heat, remove to a cold place, taking care not to disturb the crust. Leave to cool slowly. After 12 hours or so skim off the Cornish clotted cream crust using a wide bladed knife. Serve cold in a crystal glass bowl."

The cream looks particularly attractive when served in small china pots or little glass dishes. I think it always looks better to serve it up to the brim of a couple of small dishes rather than half-filling a larger dish. It all adds to that lovely bountiful feeling of extravagance and decadence!

The Jam to Serve with Scones

I must admit upfront that the most perfect jam to serve with scones and cream is homemade strawberry jam. But, I have to be honest, and admit that it's not something I have ever been particularly tempted to make. However, as lovely as homemade jam is, it is usually very sweet. Instead, I serve a good-quality strawberry conserve, which is really like a reduced-sugar jam. What I really like about using it is that, as it is less sweet, you can eat more scones and cream because it reduces the sickly factor! What I should really say, of course, is that it is a much healthier version etc. etc., but you can work that out for yourselves can't you?

Tangy Lemon Curd

Another old-fashioned, homemade treat! Although raspberry or strawberry jam is the classic filling for Victoria sandwich cake, I often like to serve it filled with homemade lemon curd. This easy recipe is cooked in the microwave oven and makes a particularly tangy curd. From start to finish, this recipe takes about 1 hour.
The timings are for a 650w microwave – adjust accordingly.

5 juicy lemons, with good skins (preferably unwaxed)	170 g (1½ sticks) butter, cut into small pieces
340 g (1⅔ cups) caster sugar (fine white sugar)	4 large free-range eggs

MAKES 3 STANDARD-SIZED JARS

1. Grate the zest from the lemons into a large, microwave-proof bowl.

2. Squeeze the juice of 2½ lemons and add to the zest, together with the sugar and butter (on average, each lemon should produce 4 Tbsp of juice). Reserve the juice of the remaining 2½ lemons.

3. Place the bowl in the microwave and cook on full heat for 1½ minutes, stir well and then cook for a further 1½ minutes. Stir thoroughly, making sure that the sugar and butter have dissolved. The timings are for a 650w microwave – adjust accordingly.

4. Use this cooking time to whisk the eggs and squeeze the juice from the remaining lemons.

5. Add the eggs and lemon juice to the mixture and microwave for 1 minute. Whisk and return to the microwave 5-6 times or until the mixture is thick enough to coat the back of a spoon. It is important to whisk well after every minute to encourage a smooth texture.

6. Pour into small warmed, sterilised jars. Cover loosely with a clean cloth and when quite cold, seal and store in the refrigerator. The curd will keep in the fridge for about six–eight weeks.

tip To make a lovely gift for friends and family, pour the curd into pretty jars and attach decorative and personalised labels.

CAKES AND BAKES

The recipes I've included here are really easy to follow and are very enjoyable to make, so have a go!

Victoria Sandwich Cake

Here is my easy-peasy, all-in-one recipe straight from my afternoon tea course. It is a traditional, jam-filled sponge cake. I've suggested using raspberry jam to fill the cake so as to have a different flavour from that of the strawberry conserve used for the scones. But if you prefer strawberry, use strawberry! Lemon curd also makes an excellent filling.

You will notice that the fat, sugar and flour are all in equal measure. This is because traditionally the baker would start with the weight of the eggs and take like amounts of the remaining ingredients to balance them. The average large egg weighs sixty grams. Accordingly, by using two, the weight is 120 grams. Because the weight of the eggs can vary, I suggest, in the recipe, that you may need to add a teaspoon or two of hot water if the mixture is not of a "soft dropping consistency". Adding the vanilla essence towards the end of the mixing time helps to keep the strength of the flavour.

120 g (1 cup) plain white flour
2 level teaspoons baking powder
Pinch of salt
120 g (⅔ cup) soft margarine
120 g (⅔ cup) white caster sugar (fine, white sugar)
2 large eggs

A few drops of vanilla extract
A teaspoon or 2 of hot, boiled water, only if necessary (*see recipe*)
4 rounded Tablespoons raspberry jam
Icing sugar (powdered, confectioner's sugar) to dust

1. Preheat the oven – conventional 180°C, 350°F gas 4 moderate

2. Prepare two 18-cm (7-in) loose-bottomed cake tins by greasing them with butter and lining the bases of each with circles of silicone paper (baking parchment).

Victoria Sandwich Cake

3. Place the flour into a small mixing bowl and stir in the baking powder.

4. Place the margarine and sugar into a separate large bowl.

5. Sieve the flour mixture into the margarine and sugar, then add the eggs (If you sieve the flour twice you will get even lighter results).

6. Preferably using an electric whisk, beat well for about 1 minute until soft and creamy. Add the vanilla extract and beat or whisk again for a (slightly shorter!) minute. The mixture should be of a soft, dropping consistency, so add a little hot water if necessary. If you are using an electric whisk or beater take care not to over beat.

> ### VARIATIONS
>
> **Orange or lemon** – mix in the finely grated zest of an orange or lemon to the creamed mixture and sandwich together with lemon curd (preferably homemade, see page 54).
>
> **Chocolate** – replace 2 rounded tablespoons of the flour with an equal amount of cocoa powder and sandwich together with cream or a chocolate filling of your choice.
>
> **Coffee** – dissolve 1 heaped teaspoon of instant coffee in a teaspoon of hot, boiled water and add to the unbeaten ingredients. Sandwich the cake together with cream or coffee-flavoured buttercream.

7. Divide the mixture equally between the tins, smooth the tops and bake for about 20–25 minutes. The cake is cooked when it is a pale golden colour and the centre of the sponge springs back into place when lightly pressed.

8. Let the cakes rest in the tins for a couple of minutes before turning them onto a wire cooling rack. (If you do this too soon the cakes will stick to the rack.) Remove the lining paper and leave to cool for a few minutes.

9. Spread the raspberry jam over one half of the cake and then place the other half on top. Sprinkle the top of the cake with sifted icing sugar (powdered confectioner's sugar) to dust. Leave to cool completely before lifting onto a plate.

Scottish Shortbread – "Petticoat Tails"

It may seem a bit fussy that I use so many different varieties of flour in this recipe, but this is what gives it that special grainy and crunchy texture that is so delicious and short-bready! And if that isn't a real word, well, I think it should be.

MAKES TWO 16.5-CM (6½-IN) ROUNDS

150 g (1¼ cup) plain white flour
50 g (¼ cup) ground rice or semolina
25 g (2 rounded tablespoons) corn flour
75 g (⅓ cup) caster sugar, (fine white sugar) plus extra for sprinkling

150 g (1⅓ sticks) butter (I use cold salted or slightly salted), but not straight from the fridge and cut into small pieces

1. You will need a 39 x 30-cm (15¼ x 12¾-in) baking sheet/tin. There is no need to grease it.

2. Place the dry ingredients into a large mixing bowl and stir thoroughly.

3. Add the butter and rub it into the dry ingredients until the mixture goes just beyond the "breadcrumb" stage and starts to cling together. Form into a ball.

4. Knead the mixture very lightly and divide into two equal balls.

5. Place the balls of dough on to the baking sheet and form into two 16.5-cm (6½-in) flat circles. Prick all over, using a fork. The purpose of this is to remove the air and stop the dough rising.

6. Use the back of a knife to mark eight equal triangles in each circle of dough. This is to facilitate cutting when the shortbread is cooked.

Scottish Shortbread or "Petticoat Tails".

VARIATIONS

Shortbread circles – I like to make very small circles of shortbread to serve with drinks or coffee after dinner. It can be hard to find a plain cutter small enough, so I usually use a small sherry glass or something similar, to get the right size.

Shortbread heart – I recently experimented by putting half the mixture into a heart-shaped cake tin and it works beautifully. It makes the perfect base for covering with whipped cream and strawberries. Delicious!

7. Using your forefinger and thumb, pinch up the edges to form a decorative (petticoat!) pattern.

8. For best results, chill the dough circles in the fridge for about 20 minutes prior to baking. Bake in a preheated oven – conventional 155°C, 300°F, gas mark 2–3 (slow to moderate) for about 30 minutes until golden brown – the colour of pale straw. (Bake for a little longer if you prefer the shortbread browner and crunchier.)

9. Sprinkle with a little extra caster sugar and cool in the tin for about 10 minutes before turning out and cutting through where marked. Place on a wire rack to cool completely. Store in an airtight container.

Cutting the Shortbread

If your memory is anything like mine, I advise you to set a timer to 10 minutes to remind you to cut the shortbread. If you cut it too soon it will be too soft and will break. If you leave it too long before cutting, it will become brittle and break.

Florentines

These crunchy little biscuits are delicious with or without the chocolate coating. I often serve some of each. They keep very well, providing you store them in an airtight container and also, come to think of it, if you hide the container very carefully!

MAKES 40 SMALL FLORENTINES

60g (½ cup) plain white flour
7 red glacé cherries
60g (⅓ cup) margarine
60g (⅓ cup) Demerara sugar
60g (3 good tablespoons) golden syrup*
90g (2 cups) flaked almonds
2 rounded teaspoons chopped mixed citrus peel
1 teaspoon lemon juice

Chocolate Coating

Approx 200g good quality thin plain chocolate (at least 70% cocoa solids) for coating the baked Florentines.
Thin chocolate is much easier to break up before melting.

1. Preheat the oven – conventional 180°C, 350°F, gas mark 4 (moderate).

2. Line baking sheets/tins with silicone paper (baking parchment). You will need 3 unless you do them in batches.

3. Weigh out the flour into a shallow dish. Roll the cherries in it and chop them. (The flour makes them less sticky and much easier to chop).

tip If using a tablespoon to measure the syrup it helps to grease it lightly first.

4. Add the citrus peel and nuts to the flour and cherries and stir well.

5. Place the margarine, sugar and syrup into a saucepan (preferably non-stick) and heat gently until melted.

Florentines

tip If golden syrup is not available: try substituting with equal parts of light corn syrup and honey or 2 parts light corn syrup and 1 part molasses

Check that the sugar has dissolved.

6. Remove from the heat and stir in the flour, cherries, nuts, mixed peel and lastly the lemon juice.

7. Drop small spoonfuls of the mixture onto the baking sheets, spacing them well apart. Flatten with a fork and bake for about 9–10 minutes until a rich golden brown. N.B. The uncooked mixture gradually tends to thicken as you are putting it onto the baking trays – don't worry – this is normal!

8. After baking, allow to harden before transferring to wire cooling racks.

9. Now you need to melt the chocolate. You can do this in two ways: either in a heatproof bowl over a pan of barely simmering water or in the microwave for about 1½ minutes, checking it quite frequently and stirring occasionally. Remember that the amount of time it takes to melt the chocolate will depend on the type of microwave oven that you have. The timings are for a 650w microwave – adjust accordingly. The important thing is not to heat the chocolate for too long otherwise it will spoil. Greasing the bowl with a little butter before adding the chocolate helps to stop the chocolate from sticking to the bowl too much.

10. Coat the flat side of the Florentines with the melted chocolate and mark with the back of a fork to create wavy lines. It's a sticky business!

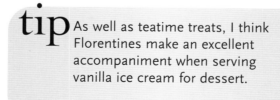

tip As well as teatime treats, I think Florentines make an excellent accompaniment when serving vanilla ice cream for dessert.

Maids of Honour

This historic little tart is curd-filled, flavoured with lemon and enriched with ground almonds. The original recipe for this longstanding speciality remains a closely-kept secret, so this is my own version of these delicious treats.

MAKES 24 TARTLETS

200 g (1 block) ready-made puff pastry (even the chefs use ready-made puff pastry nowadays!)

Zest of 1 small lemon

1 large egg

225 g (1 scant cup) curd cheese, pour off any surface liquid

50 g (½ cup) ground almonds (preferably freshly ground)

40 g (3 level tablespoons) caster sugar (fine white sugar)

2 teaspoons lemon juice or brandy

Approx. 4 tablespoons Lemon curd (preferably homemade, *see page* 54)

Nutmeg (preferably freshly grated) to sprinkle over the tartlets before baking.

Icing sugar (powdered confectioner's sugar) to dust

1. Preheat the oven – conventional 200°C, 400°F, gas mark 6 (moderately hot).

2. Roll out the pastry as thinly as possible on a lightly floured surface. Use an 8-cm (3¼-in) cutter to cut out 24 rounds of pastry. Line 24 shallow, un-greased bun tins with the pastry and leave to rest.

3. To make the topping, place the lemon zest, egg, curd cheese, almonds, sugar and lemon juice or brandy in a bowl and whisk well.

4. Spoon ½ teaspoon of lemon curd into each pastry case and cover completely with the topping mixture. Sprinkle with nutmeg.

5. Bake for 8 minutes, then reduce the heat – conventional 180°C, 350°F, gas mark 4

Maids of Honour

(moderate)– and cook for a further 10 minutes.

6. Cool slightly on a wire rack and dust with icing sugar (powdered confectioner's sugar). The tarts are best served warm. If you are serving the tarts some time after you've baked them, you can always pop them in a hot oven briefly, or heat them in the microwave for a few seconds.

History of the Maids of Honour Recipe

The original Maids of Honour are reputed to have been created nearly 300 years ago. Henry VIII is said to have named them when he discovered his wife, Anne Boleyn, and her maids of honour eating the tarts from a silver dish. Legend has it that Henry liked them so much that he had the secret recipe locked in an iron box and that the unfortunate maid who invented them, was imprisoned and ordered to produce the pastries solely for the royal household! By the eighteenth century the recipe had been disclosed to a bakery and the cakes became a popular teatime feature in fashionable society.

The Original Maids of Honour Tea House was opened in the early eighteenth century by Robert Newens, in Kew, Surrey. Today, it is still a family-run business and the secret recipe is as closely-guarded as ever.

Gingerbread Men and Women! (and boys and girls!)

Here's a fun recipe, the results of which will be particularly appreciated by smaller visitors! You don't have to make people shapes, you could use any shaped cutter that you like. It's great to serve gingerbread at Christmas time, cut into festive shapes. The amount of gingerbread men this recipe makes depends on the size of cutter you use.

40 g (2 good tablepoons) black treacle or use dark molasses	2 level teaspoons ground ginger
75 g (4 tablespoons) golden syrup (*see tip on page* 64)	1 rounded teaspoon ground cinnamon
	½ teaspoon bicarbonate of soda (baking soda)
75 g (½ cup, well-packed) soft brown sugar (light or dark)	100 g (½ cup) margarine
Zest of 1 orange	Approx. 225 g (1¾ cups) plain white flour
1 tablespoon fresh orange juice	Glacé cherries and raisins to decorate

1. Preheat the oven – conventional 180°C, 350°F, gas mark 4 (moderate). Prepare baking sheets/tins, by greasing them or lining them with silicone paper (baking parchment).

2. Put the treacle, syrup, sugar, orange zest, orange juice and spices into a medium-sized saucepan. Place on a medium heat and stir, while bringing to the boil.

3. Remove from the heat and stir in the bicarbonate of soda and margarine.

4. Gradually add enough of the flour to make a smooth, pliable dough, using a wooden spoon. Leave to cool for about 30 minutes.

5. On a lightly floured board, roll out the dough to a thickness of about 3 mm (⅛ in) and cut out the gingerbread people.

6. Now it's time to have even more fun! Cut up the raisins and cherries to make the eyes, mouth and coat buttons. Remember to make them smile!

7. Place on the prepared baking sheets/tins and bake for about 10–15 minutes, until firm to the touch. Transfer to a wire rack to cool.

Other Decorating Ideas

Some people like to ice the cooked biscuits with glacé icing. If making little Christmas tree shapes, you can create a pretty snow effect by outlining them with white glacé icing. Glacé icing is simply made by mixing icing sugar (powdered confectioner's sugar) with hot, boiled water.

Carrot Cake

One of my children is particularly "anti-carrots" and when he was little, this recipe proved

Approx 500 g carrots (8 medium-sized carrots)
100 g (1 cup) walnut pieces
375 g (3 cups) plain white flour
1½ level teaspoons baking powder
1 level teaspoon bicarbonate of soda (baking soda)
1 rounded teaspoon ground nutmeg

¼ teaspoon (rounded) ground cloves
1½ rounded teaspoons ground cinnamon
Pinch of salt
4 large eggs
300 g (2 cups well-packed) soft brown sugar
350 ml (1⅓ cups) sunflower oil

FOR THE TOPPING:

250 g cream cheese (e.g. Philadelphia®)
110 g icing sugar, (powdered confectioner's sugar) sieved
Zest of 1 lemon

Few drops of vanilla extract
Fresh lemon juice to taste
Handful of walnuts, toasted and finely chopped (optional)

Carrot Cake

to be an excellent way of getting him to receive all the benefits of this nutritious vegetable, without the hassle and fuss!

1. Prepare a 25-cm spring-form pan – grease and line the bottom with a circle of silicone paper or baking parchment. Dust with flour.

2. Preheat the oven – conventional 170°C, 325°F, gas mark 3 (moderate).

3. Peel and coarsely grate the carrots. Roughly chop the walnuts (not too finely) about pea sized is good!

4. Measure the flour into a medium sized bowl, then add the baking powder, bicarbonate of soda, nutmeg, cloves and cinnamon. Stir well and set aside.

5. In a separate large mixing bowl, whisk together the eggs and the sugar until they thicken (about 3–4 minutes) and then and then gradually add the oil, whisking all the time.

6. Add the grated carrots and nuts to the egg, sugar and oil mixture and stir.

7. Sieve the flour and spice mixture directly into the carrot mixture (add any spices that remain in the sieve) and using a large spoon, fold in carefully, to preserve all the air that has been whisked in.

8. Pour the mixture into the prepared tin and bake for 1 hour–1 hour 10 minutes. The cake should be nicely risen, firm to the touch and beginning to shrink away from the edges of the tin.

9. Leave in the tin for about 15 minutes before turning out on to a wire cake rack to cool completely before adding the topping.

10. To make the topping: Beat together the cream cheese and icing sugar (powdered con-

fectioner's sugar) and gradually add the lemon zest and vanilla extract. Add a little lemon juice to taste. Do not add too much as this will make the mixture too soft.

11. Use a palette knife to spread the topping on to the cake. Sprinkle with chopped walnuts if liked.

TEA BREADS

I think the best way to describe these is to say that they are a cross between cake and bread. They very often contain fruit of some kind and can be served sliced, spread with butter or just as they are.

There is something very comforting and "olde worlde" about tea breads. They remind me of the days when village bakeries used to have their own particular specialities of these delicious treats. Even more precious to me is the memory of visiting my favourite aunt, Auntie Edna, who was a wonderful cook. The smell of tea breads baking in her kitchen always served as a wonderful welcome whenever we went to visit.

Malt loaves are available to buy in the bread department of supermarkets, but to my mind, nothing quite compares to the flavour and texture of something that has been homemade! Over the following pages are three of my favourite teabread recipes.

Spicy Date, Apricot and Nut Loaf

100 g (½ cup) margarine or butter

150 g (½ cup) golden syrup

50 g (3 tablespoons) malt extract

2 large eggs

150 ml (5 fl. oz/approx ⅔ cup) milk

225 g (1¾ cups) plain flour

1 level teaspoon bicarbonate of soda
(baking soda)

2 level teaspoons powdered ginger

1 level teaspoon powdered cinnamon

50g (½ cup) walnuts, chopped

75 g (½ cup) dried dates, chopped and pitted

4 or 5 whole dried apricots

1.   Preheat the oven to 150°C, 300°F, gas mark 2 (slow) and then butter and line a loaf tin. Base 19 x 8.5cm (7½in x 3½in). Top 21 x 11cm (8½in x 4½in).

2.   Place the margarine (or butter), syrup and malt into a medium sized saucepan and melt over a low heat. Remove from the heat and allow to cool in the pan.

3.   Meanwhile, chop the apricots quite small and set aside.

4.   Mix together the flour and bicarbonate of soda and sieve into a large bowl. Add the ginger and cinnamon and stir into the flour mixture, together with the chopped nuts and ⅔ of the dates and chopped apricots.

5.   Whisk the eggs. Add the milk and whisk again.

6.   Pour the egg and milk mixture into the syrup mixture (in the now cooled pan) and stir well before pouring into the flour mixture. Stir well to combine.

7.   Pour into the prepared tin, sprinkling the remaining ⅓ of the dates and apricots evenly over the top.

8.   Bake for approx. 1 hour and 10 minutes.

9.   Test for "doneness" by inserting a small wooden cocktail stick in the centre – if it comes away clean then the cake is properly cooked – if not, return for a few more minutes.

10.   Leave to cool in the baking tin for approx. 30 minutes, before turning out onto a wire cooling rack.

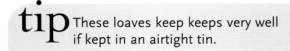

tip These loaves keep keeps very well if kept in an airtight tin.

Banana Bread

I can never think of banana bread without it reminding me of my friend Catherine, who makes the best version of this delicious bread that I have ever tasted. She has definitely got the right touch!

250 g (2 cups) plain flour	120 g (⅔ cup) soft margarine
2 level teaspoons baking powder	120 g (½ cup) castor sugar (fine white
1 rounded teaspoon bicarbonate of soda	sugar)
(baking soda)	2 large eggs
½ teaspoon salt	4 large peeled, over-ripe bananas – about
1 level teaspoon cinnamon	425 grams (2⅓ cups)

1.   Preheat the oven – conventional 170°C, 325°F, gas mark 3 (moderate).

2.   Grease a 23 x 13-cm (9 x 5-in) loaf tin and line it with baking parchment or silicone paper.

3.   Measure the flour, bicarbonate of soda and salt and cinnamon into a bowl and stir well.

Banana Bread

Set aside.

4. Peel and mash the bananas and set aside.

5. Place eggs in a separate bowl and whisk well.

6.   (Preferably using an electric whisk or beater) cream the margarine and sugar together in a large bowl until light and fluffy.

7.   Gradually add the beaten eggs to the margarine and sugar, while continuing to whisk or beat.

8.   Add the mashed bananas and stir gently.

9.   Place flour mixture in to a sieve and gradually add to the banana mixture, stirring gently until it is all incorporated. (Don't be tempted to beat or whisk at this stage, or you will lose all the air that you so carefully created in steps 5 and 6.)

10.   Pour the mixture into the prepared loaf tin.

11.   Bake in the oven for 30 minutes, reducing the temperature to conventional 155°C, 300°F, gas mark 2–3 (slow to moderate) – for a further 40 minutes or so. It is cooked when a wooden cocktail stick inserted into the centre of the loaf comes out clean.

12.   Allow the bread to cool in the tin for about 10 minutes before turning out onto a wire rack.

If possible, allow 24 hours before serving. This allows for the texture to firm up and for the flavours to develop.

"No Fat, Sugar or Egg" – Fruit Loaf

"No Fat, Sugar or Egg" Fruit Loaf;

This is a particularly good recipe for anyone with allergies or simply for anyone trying to avoid added sugar. I have also found it to be very popular with very young children, for whom it can be cut into bite sized pieces. It does tend to use rather a lot of dried fruit, so be sure to stock up.

225 g (1½ cups) dates, chopped and pitted

300 ml (1⅓ cups) cold water

170 g (1⅓ cups) flour (I use half whole-wheat and half plain white flour)

1 rounded teaspoon baking powder

450 g (3½ cups) mixed dried fruit (raisins, sultanas, currants etc.)

1 level teaspoon mixed spice

Zest of 1 orange

4 Tablespoons fresh orange juice

55 g (½ cup) ground almonds

1. Grease a 900-g (2-1b) loaf tin and line with with baking parchment or silicone paper.

2. Preheat the oven – conventional 155°C, 350°F gas Mark 2–3 (slow to moderate).

3. Place the dates and water into a saucepan and cook gently until the dates are soft. Remove from the heat and allow to cool. Alternatively soak in cold water overnight.

4. Place the flour and baking powder into a large mixing bowl and stir well.

5. Add the cooled, soaked dates and all the other ingredients. Mix together well.

6. Mix together well before spooning into the prepared loaf tin and bake for approximately 1 hour 20 minutes. The loaf is cooked when a wooden cocktail stick inserted into the centre of the loaf comes out clean. Allow to cool for a few minutes in the tin, before cooling on a wire rack.

tip Because of the high fruit content, this loaf keeps very well. I like to wrap it in cling film (Saran wrap) first and then in silver foil. Store in the fridge.

PART 2
The Tea Chest

CHAPTER 5

Tea – From Plantation to Pot

EFORE WE GO ANY FURTHER – let's just stop for a few moments and look at the origins of this "magical little leaf" that has had such an influence worldwide and which, of course, takes centre stage at afternoon tea parties. The information in this chapter isn't exhaustive and it won't teach you how to become an expert tea taster. However, it will give you the basics so that you understand, and perhaps appreciate a little more, how the tea gets from the plantation to your pot, and why it tastes the way it does.

WHAT IS TEA?

Tea is an aromatic stimulant, containing tannic compounds (not to be confused with tannic acid, which is used in tanning leather), technically named polyphenols. It also contains small quantities of vitamins A, B2, C and D, various trace minerals, essential oils and, of course, caffeine.

It is the tannin compounds and essential oils which are, in the main, responsible for the flavour, colour, astringency (dryness) and aroma. Together, they produce the "high, medium and base notes" of tea that are referred to by expert tea tasters.

Tea comes from the dried leaves of the tea bush *Camellia Sinensis*, which is native to South East Asia. It is a much-branched, evergreen shrub and comes from the same family as the beautiful *Camellia Japonica*. When in bloom, *Camellia Sinensis* produces a profusion of scented white or pinkish blossoms, with thick waxy petals. Although we refer to "tea bushes", they are actually trees that are trimmed down to a convenient height for the tea to be picked. If allowed to grow to its true height, the tea tree can grow to a height of 15.25 metres (50 feet). Severe pruning not only cuts down the size, but also ensures that the energy of the plant is concentrated in the leaves. Only the delicate young leaves (the tips) and buds are used and a well cared for tea bush will go on yielding for 50 years or more.

Surprisingly, although there are many different types of tea, they all derive from this same plant. The differences in taste and colour all depend on soil, climate, altitude, harvesting and oxidisation. The best tea tends to come from tea estates situated on high ground. The temperature is cooler and this encourages the slow growth of small leaves in contrast to the thick and coarser growth of the hot lowlands. For example, there are important tea-growing areas in the central hills of Sri Lanka and the famous Darjeeling tea is produced in the foothills of the Himalayas in India.

Once the tea tree has reached maturity, the leaves are harvested four to five times a year. When the plant begins a growth spurt or "flush", the picking is carefully timed to ensure that the leaves are large enough and in optimum condition.

In most tea-producing countries, the labour-intensive method of picking, drying, crushing and oxidising tea has been used for centuries. The plucked leaves are collected in a basket or bag and carried on the back of the plucker. When the basket is full, it is taken to a collection point to be weighed and then taken to the factory for processing, or "making", as tea manufacture is known in the trade. The production process involved depends on the type of tea that is being made.

A New Way to Pick Tea Leaves?

Some growers have had success using a machine that works rather like a vacuum cleaner, sucking the leaves off the branches. This method is used for the cheaper varieties of tea, as it is not capable of discriminating between the high quality tip leaves and the coarser leaves towards the bottom of the branch.

There are many grades of tea. The grading system relates to the size of the leaf and not to their quality. Teas grown on the various estates and at various times of the year, are all slightly different. In order to maintain a uniform standard, teas from as many as 20 or 30 different estates are mixed together to produce a reliable and consistent end result, that passes the taste test.

VARIETIES OF TEA

There are four basic types of tea: black, green, oolong and white. The famous Twinings tea company aptly compares black tea to red wine, oolong to rosé and green and white tea to white wine. There are also blended teas and flavoured and scented teas. I just want to clarify a point here that the herbal teas that have become so popular in recent years are not actually "teas" in the strict sense of the word, as they do not contain the leaves of the *Camellia Sinensis* plant. They are herbal infusions, which are also known as "tisanes".

TEA TASTING NOTES

In the process of my research, I came across this really helpful guide to tea tasting written by the Twinings tea company who have been in this business since 1706. Their shop and museum in the Strand, London, U.K. is well worth a visit. I hope you enjoy the slightly tongue- in-cheek approach in which they are written and find them as helpful and amusing as I do. I also love the way they describe some of my favourite black teas – namely: Assam, Ceylon, Darjeeling, Earl Grey and English Breakfast. I've also included their description of Lapsang Souchong, simply because it is too good to leave out. Who could resist a 'tea with whiskers'…?!

Key Tasting Terms

- **Sweetness** – tasted at the tip of the tongue and tastes sugary.
- **Acidity** – sensed on the sides of the tongue.
- **Tannin** – tasted at the back of the tongue and tastes bitter like a strong cup of tea. Also has a drying effect on the gums. It comes from the phenolic compounds of the tea leaf and is particularly prominent in black teas.
- **Length** – length is how long you taste the tea once you have swallowed. It gives an indication of quality – the longer the length, the higher the quality.
- **Body** – weight and fullness of tea on the palate.
- **Balance** – when all of the tea's component parts blend together. This is the most important indication of quality.

BLACK TEA

Black teas are oxidised, which means that the leaves are exposed to the air for a precise length of time, in order to allow natural chemical reactions to occur. In the process, the

Black, or is it Red Tea?

In Chinese, and culturally-related languages, black tea is known as red tea, which is perhaps a more accurate description of the colour of the liquid it produces. However, in the Western world, "red tea" more commonly refers to South African rooibos tea, which is a herbal tisane.

leaves change colour from green to copper and the flavour is intensified.

There are four basic steps involved in the production of black tea: withering, rolling, oxidising and firing (or drying). The "orthodox" method produces larger particles of leaf and is used for most high quality leaf teas. The "CTC" (cut, tear and curl) method produces smaller leaf particles that give a stronger and quicker brew. This type of tea is mostly used to make tea bags. The caffeine content of black tea is generally the highest of all the tea types. Examples of black teas include English Breakfast, Assam, Darjeeling, Ceylon, Earl Grey and Lapsang Souchang. Here's how they are wittily described by Twinings.

ENGLISH BREAKFAST

"A yeoman – an old English oak of a tea"

BREWING/SERVING INSTRUCTIONS:

Brew with freshly boiled water for three to five minutes. Can be drunk black or with milk.

APPEARANCE:

Amontillado sherry – a lovely, pale, sunny golden tea with tinges of green and rich amber.

NOSE:

Smells of sweet, spring, juicy green grass.

TASTE:

Savoury, slightly nutty character and a flicker of fruitiness on the palate that then immediately fades. An obvious tannic structure – but with attractive, slightly sweet elements that are reminiscent of the vanilla/coconut group of flavours. The finish is quite creamy – even before you've actually poured milk in. Even a tiny amount of milk enhances the blend's creaminess and brings out fruitiness at the very end. When you leave English Breakfast to cool, the fruit comes through even more strongly.

MOOD/OCCASION:

The name says it all! You don't want anything too delicate first thing in the morning and English Breakfast is nice and burly. The full bodied strength of English Breakfast with its ever so slightly abrasive edge is exactly what you want in "a wake myself up" kind of tea. It's definitely a tea you'd serve in a sturdy mug while still in your pyjamas – bracing yourself to start the day.

FOOD MATCH:

A good old fashioned fry up – or at the very least, a bacon or sausage sandwich.

COUNTRY OF ORIGIN:

A blend of teas from several continents.

INTERESTING FACT:

This tea was originally blended to complement the traditional hearty English Breakfast from which its name is derived. However, the refreshing taste of English Breakfast makes it a popular tea to drink at any time when you feel in need of a lift. Twinings also offers Organic and Decaffeinated English Breakfast blends.

🫖 ASSAM

"A great mid morning blend with a crease in its trousers"

BREWING/SERVING INSTRUCTIONS:

Brew with freshly boiled water for three to five minutes. Best served with milk. A smidgeon of sugar would work well with Assam - it would enhance the flavours rather than muddy them.

LOOK:

Golden syrup with a tinge of russet red.

NOSE:

Creamy and malty – an enveloping, "hug" of a tea with a warming, rounded tea fragrance.

TASTE:

A strong, uncomplicated tea which reflects its "single origin" status. A lovely, thick-mouth feel with more fruit at its heart than English Breakfast. A tiny hint of grapeyness comes through when savouring the flavour and its fruit heart is rather dry and stoney. Tannin comes through right at the end and is slightly more grainy than the creamy finish of English Breakfast. The initial direct and robust flavours soften when the tea cools. More fruit comes through with a raisin richness to it.

MOOD/OCCASION:

An hour or so after English Breakfast when you're suited and booted, if not already immersed, in the beginnings of the day. While English Breakfast wakes you up, Assam has the ability to make the eyes widen a little further, refresh the senses and avoid a potential mid morning slump.

FOOD MATCHES:

The perfect tea for biscuit dunking! This blend would also work perfectly with sesame toast. With its surprising hidden depths when cool, Assam would also work with ice – although its consistency wouldn't lend itself to a transparent result – the taste would be absolutely delicious.

COUNTRY OF ORIGIN:

North East India – from the flood plains of Brahmaputra.

INTERESTING FACT:

The conditions in the Brahmaputra Valley – its low elevation, high rainfall and high humidity – are responsible for Assam's unique flavour. Assam is the tea you are most likely to be served in India – and with lots of milk and sugar.

🫖 DARJEELING

"Tremendous company – leaves you with a lingering smile"

BREWING/SERVING INSTRUCTIONS:

Brew with freshly boiled water for three to five minutes. Better without milk – or at most just a dash.

APPEARANCE:

Beautiful to look at – a light golden, green colour.

NOSE:

You really get a nose from this blend – beautiful Muscatel and honey – yet there's no direct sweetness. A fabulous fragrance that elicits images of high luscious mountains. Fresh, savoury, lettucy, green creamy fragrance – like the very heart of a sweet Cos lettuce over-laid with a veil of grapeyness. You can even smell a dark gold, coppery richness to the tannin of this blend. Although technically you can't smell tannin, already your mouth is being prepared. Very evocative.

TASTE:

When first hitting the palate, almost jalapeno pepper and half the elements of a good black peppercorn – with none of the heat. It certainly stops you in your tracks. Crisp with the gentle tannin of a white grape. Like in wine when you remove the sweetness of the Muscatel grape so that you're left with flavour stripped to the bone. A mild, very sophisticated tannin which has a sheen and polish – unlike some other tannins which can be greasier. This behaves like a tip top wine with long mouth feel – it lingers on the palate for a minute or two. The peppery start disappears and the flavour evolves with a delicious velvety and richness coming through and the continued aromatic qualities of Jalapeno.

MOOD/OCCASION:

You'd serve this sophisticated tea to the vicar in the old days. There's no doubt this is a thoughtful tea, you're inspired to contemplate the flavours and aromatic experiences it offers. Elegant and interesting – the flavours just go on and on – and leave you with fond memories long after you've drunk it.

FOOD:

Darjeeling stands very well alone without food. However, a soft, creamy cheese with jalapeno or a slightly hot salsa would work very well with this blend.

COUNTRY OF ORIGIN:

North east India – from the foothills of the Himalayas.

INTERESTING FACT:

Darjeeling represents just one per cent of India's tea crops – which is one of the reasons why it is so revered. It can also only be picked between the months of April to October. As a result, it's much fought over among tea buyers – especially First Flush Darjeeling – plucked in April and considered the highest quality Darjeeling of all. The high altitude, soil and climate of Darjeeling's tea gardens all contribute towards the unique flavours of this tea.

CEYLON

"A bit of a rough diamond who speaks his mind"

BREWING/SERVING INSTRUCTIONS:

Brew with freshly boiled water for three to five minutes. Drink black, with a little milk or with lemon.

APPEARANCE:

A light but rich, clean amber with hints of pale ginger.

NOSE:

Succulent grass on a summer's day that's incredibly enticing.

TASTE:

A surprising blend – more powerful and less delicate than expected. Tiny elements of orange rind when it first hits the palate and slightly citrus in a way that's aromatic and slightly bitter. Hints of fresh tobacco come through – lots of unusual and interesting flavours bound together in a terribly elegant result The tannin is less silky than Darjeeling with a slight barkiness that grips the palate and then rounds off to a dry finish.

MOOD/OCCASION:

Similar to 1706, Ceylon lends itself to a contemplative mood, when you're taking stock – but also inclined to shoot from the hip. You're in the mood for something solid and honest, nothing too fancy.

FOOD:

Lemon would be very complementary and freshen up/sharpen the orange elements of this blend – after all, orange and lemon is a classic marriage of flavours. Toast with Cornish butter and a dark, full bodied marmalade would be a perfect match for Ceylon.

COUNTRY OF ORIGIN:

Sri Lanka.

INTERESTING FACT:

In the 1870s, Ceylon became a major tea producing area after a coffee crop failed. It's tea is still referred to as Ceylon, despite the country changing its name to Sri Lanka in 1972 when it became independent.

AROMATICS

Richly scented and highly individual, Twinings' delicate, floral and aromatic teas provide an unforgettable sensory experience.

EARL GREY

"Soft, mellow and charming – with a bit of an edge on closer inspection"

BREWING/SERVING INSTRUCTIONS:

Brew for three to five minutes, using freshly boiled water. Drink black, with a little milk or with lemon.

APPEARANCE:

A light, vibrant tea of pale gold with a hint of bronze.

NOSE:

A very fragrant tea that hints of fruit and floral ingredients. The fruit bouquet is citrus – especially lime – like smelling a lime's skin rather than scratching it with your finger – it's not too over-powering.

TASTE:

A very smooth blend with a fantastic, natural balance between the bergamot and the tea leaves themselves – not easy to achieve. The bergamot is rather delicate: a veil of perfume on top of the tea's flavour. You then pick up the benefits of the tannin and the sweetness of the tea. You can even derive a slight smokiness so often associated with China teas. It literally makes the mouth water. When left to cool, the tea evolves in combination with the citrus elements of the blend – gorgeously fragrant and lively.

MOOD/OCCASION:

Definitely a more sophisticated mood. Out comes the good china with this one, when you want to reward yourself or impress others. Picture yourself sitting down in a rather formal armchair – dressed up reasonably smartly and on your best behaviour! There's no question, Earl Grey draws you in with its very attractive scent but on closer inspection, there're something much more interesting. It's a little more challenging than expected, a little prickly in a very magnetic way.

FOOD:

Iced fairy cakes with crystallised violet pieces on top or any sweet cake or confectionery which has elements of violet. Earl Grey would also sit very well with mild, crumbly English cheeses such as Lancashire, Wensleydale – or even a strong, authentic English cheddar. The combination of creaminess with a slight acidity would work very well for a welsh rarebit – with the tiniest smearing of an apple and walnut chutney or a conservative dash of Worcester sauce.

COUNTRY OF ORIGIN:

Predominantly China, scented with oil from the citrus bergamot fruit (similar to an orange).

INTERESTING FACT:

"There is no doubt in my mind that Charles, the second Earl Grey, asked Twinings tea merchants to blend this special tea for him back in the early nineteenth century – resulting in the blend that is so popular today," says Stephen Twining, world-renowned tea expert and a tenth generation member of the Twining family.

⚗ LAPSANG SOUCHONG

"A tea with whiskers striding the moors with purpose"

BREWING/SERVING INSTRUCTIONS:

Brew with freshly boiled water for three to five minutes. Drink black or with a little milk.

APPEARANCE:

A rich, golden tea.

NOSE:

Mid winter and totally distinctive. A smoky fragrance that conjures up images of bonfires with a hint of pine.

TASTE:

The aroma is completely different to its taste. A very elegant flavour perfectly balanced with a delicate smokiness. There's a light, caramelised, rustic burnt oak flavour and the elements of pinewood are slightly sweet. A blend that straddles two worlds — very country but very city too.

MOOD/OCCASION:

Take Lapsang Souchong in a flask — it's an outdoor tea — perfect for cold, wet and blustering conditions.

It's incredibly evocative — with autumnal flavours: bonfires and chopping wood. It's not a fresh, bright, or happy go lucky tea — it's got purpose and is business-like. In fact, a slightly short tempered man striding the moors comes to mind when drinking this.

FOOD:

Lapsang Souchong would make a fabulous hot toddy served with heather honey and a dash of whisky — and maybe just a dash of lemon. Smoked fish would also work well — eels or mackerel as the blend's tannin would successfully cut through the oiliness.

OOLONG TEA

Oolong teas are a cross between green and black teas. The leaves are only partially oxidised, which means that they are processed for a shorter period of time than black teas. As they are only partly oxidized, they are stronger than green teas but more delicate than fully-oxidized black teas. They are produced principally in China and Taiwan, which is still often referred to as Formosa in the tea world. The Formosa oolongs tend to be oxidized for longer than those from China and are therefore blacker in appearance. Oolongs are always made from whole leaves; the leaves are never broken by rolling. The taste is "…smoother than black tea but less fresh-tasting than green tea". Examples of oolong teas are Black Dragon, Cantonese, Formosa and Jade.

Notes: Oolongs are usually drunk without milk.

GREEN TEA

These are largely unoxidized teas and the leaves are processed immediately after picking. They are air-dried (withered) and then either pan-fired (common in China) or steamed (common in Japan) to deactivate the enzyme involved in oxidisation. Because of this, green tea retains its natural olive green colour and all of its natural tannin. It also contains useful amounts of vitamin C, chlorophyll and minerals. The caffeine content is generally low but there are exceptions. Virtually all green teas come from China, Japan and Taiwan. Examples of green teas include Kangra Green, Gunpowder and Darjeeling Green.

Notes: Because of its slightly bitter taste, green tea is not usually drunk on an empty stomach. It is particularly suited to being served after a sweet dessert and is always served without milk. It is worth noting here that unlike black teas, green tea should be made with water that is slightly below boiling point. When made with boiling water it can taste very bitter.

A Closer Look at Japanese Green Teas

Sencha: This is the generic Japanese name for green tea but the term does not apply to Gyokuro.

Gyokuro: This is the most highly valued Japanese tea and is also known as Pearl Dew. The Japanese Spider Leg tea is a variety of Gyokuro. It is fired in bamboo baskets and the leaves turn out long and thin, hence its name.

Genmaicha: This is made from green tea blended with toasted rice. It is sometimes called "popcorn tea" because of its unusual taste. It is often served in Japanese restaurants.

Gunpowder: So named because of the appearance of the individually rolled leaves, which resemble pellets or gunpowder grains. It is "a strong-bodied green tea with hints of sweet and earthy flavours. It produces a medium colour green liquid".

Hojicha: Made from toasted green tea leaves. It is the green tea with the most body, and has a taste reminiscent of almost-burnt toast. It produces an amber or light brown liquid.

Matcha: This is the powdered tea used in the Japanese tea ceremony. It is called Tencha before it is powdered.

WHITE TEA

This rather exclusive, unoxidised tea is produced mostly in China and Sri Lanka, but there is also some production in the Darjeeling region of India. The processing of white tea is similar to that of green tea, but it is harvested differently. The leaves are picked when the buds are still covered by fine white "hair" – hence the name. Because the leaves are sun-dried rather than oxidized, it produces a pale brew.

White tea must be harvested at a certain time of day and during certain seasons. This tends to account for the high price that it commands. This tea is much lighter and sweeter than green tea and, generally, is even lower in caffeine.

Examples of white tea include Flowery White Pekoe, Noble Beauty, Golden Moon, White Peony and White Cloud. Yin Zhen from China is the most exotic and expensive white tea and is harvested by the imperial plucking method. This is where only the bud and first leaf are harvested; in the case of Yin Zhen it is actually only the bud that is used.

It is also possible to obtain flavoured white tea, and varieties available include liquorice, melon and ginger.

Notes: Just as with green tea, the water used to make white tea should be below boiling point. The tea should be infused for up to 6 minutes to allow the buds to open and release their full flavour. When serving, remember that it is meant to be light in colour and aroma and is served without milk.

Because of the delicate flavour, it is not advisable to serve white tea with highly-spiced food. A subtle and soothing drink, white tea has been described as "...a non-alcoholic answer to fine wine". Because of the low caffeine content, it is very suitable for serving in the evening after dinner.

FLAVOURED AND SCENTED TEAS

It seems likely that adding flavour and/or scent to teas was initially introduced as a clever way of disguising poor quality tea. However, as consumers are becoming more and more discerning, this is less likely to be the case and some very reputable tea merchants are producing very high quality flavoured and scented teas.

Innumerable flavourings are added to a base tea that may be black, green, oolong or white. Some of the most popular flavourings are vanilla, orange blossom, jasmine, lemon, orange, clove and of course bergamot orange (see Earl Grey page 90).

Lapsang Souchong is one of the most coveted scented teas. The leaves are fired over smoking pine needles and this produces the distinguished smoky flavour and aroma. The best varieties are not overwhelmed by the smoke but retain some subtlety.

Notes: Scented and flavoured teas are not generally served at afternoon tea, with the exception of Earl Grey, which is suitable for drinking at any time of day.

Blended Teas

The practice of blending teas began around 1860–70, when tea merchants such as Twinings, blended different varieties of tea from various regions in order to consistently achieve a stable and uniform taste. For example, Twinings English Breakfast Blend has essentially tasted the same for decades. Blending teas made excellent business sense, because the customer knew that the taste would be consistent and would thus be more likely to go back for more!

Fortnum and Mason Royal Blend

This is a specially selected blend of Assam and Ceylon and is very refreshing. It has a smooth, almost honey-like flavour and it takes milk well. It was first blended for King Edward VII (who reigned 1901–1910) in 1902, when the British Empire was at its zenith.

Fortnum and Mason have the Royal Warrant to supply H.R.H. The Prince of Wales as Tea Merchants and Grocers.

Fortnum and Mason, the famous store in Piccadilly, London.

CHAPTER 6

The History of Tea and its Arrival in England

IN THIS CHAPTER I BRIEFLY GO RIGHT BACK to the beginning and take a look at the very origins of tea and its use, then give you a potted history of how tea arrived in England and how it became such a fundamental part of the culture.

Who Discovered Tea?

Tea has the distinction of being the most ancient beverage in the world but its exact origins are lost in antiquity. Since the whole subject of tea is surrounded by legend and differing stories, you won't be surprised to learn that the circumstances of its initial discovery are no exception to this.

We know that the Chinese have been drinking tea for the last 5,000 years and, according to Chinese legend, the Emperor Shen Nung a herbalist and teacher, was the first to discover it in 2737 BC. The Emperor is thought to have been very concerned about health and sensibly insisted that all drinking water should be boiled as a protective measure.

According to this legend, while he was travelling across his lands, the fire lit by his servants to heat up his water was made of camellia branches. Magically, some of the leaves blew into the bubbling water and the Emperor was said to have been captivated by their aroma. Despite his tendency for hypochondria, he was moved to taste it and found it to be very refreshing. He felt it to be both exhilarating and relaxing and was keen to encourage others to experience this elevated sense of wellbeing!

An Indian legend attributes the discovery of tea to Prince Bodhi-Dharma, who was a Buddhist missionary monk instrumental in bringing Buddhism from India to China and Japan. He decided to go on a seven-year meditation, during which time he vowed that he would never sleep.

Needless to say, as time progressed, he became overcome with tiredness. This legend has it that in 543 BC, he, by chance, chewed some leaves from an unknown bush and they renewed his spirits and helped him keep his vow. The bush was of course, a *camellia sinensis*.

The Japanese legend also concerns Prince Bodhi-Dharma and his quest for a long and sleepless meditation. However it differs a little, in that it is said that he failed to resist sleep and became so intolerant of his weakness that he punished himself by ripping off his eye-lids and burying them! The story tells how he returned to the exact same spot where he buried his eyelids, only to find that a tea bush had taken root. He discovered that chewing the leaves cured his fatigue and enabled him to continue with his meditation.

Who Wrote the First Book on Tea?

In 780 AD, a Chinese man, Lu Yu, wrote the first definitive book on tea, the *Ch'a Ching*. The book covers all aspects of tea – from growing to drinking. Abandoned as a child, Lu Yu was adopted by the abbot of a Zen monastery. Although greatly influenced by the Zen traditions, he went on to pursue the more poetic and scholarly ways of the Confucian tradition. His book projected him into near sainthood within his own lifetime and he became a close friend of the Emperor. It was this form of serving tea that Zen Buddhist missionaries would later introduce to imperial Japan.

Tea Comes to Japan

It was in 805 AD that tea was first introduced to Japan by Zen Buddhist missionaries who had been studying in China. They particularly prized tea for its meditation-enhancing properties. It received almost instant imperial sponsorship and spread rapidly from the royal court and monasteries to other sections of Japanese society.

Tea was gradually elevated to an art form, resulting in the creation of Chanoyu – the Japanese tea ceremony. Writer and scholar, Okakura Kakuzo, wrote in 1906, "Teaism is a cult founded on the adoration of the beautiful among the sordid facts of everyday existence. It inculcates purity and harmony, the mystery of mutual charity, the romanticism of the social order."

Tea Arrives in England

Ironically, despite having become so closely associated with tea, the British, were, in fact, the last of the seafaring nations to actually taste it. Tea was first brought to England by the Dutch, who exported it from China via Japan. At this time, in around 1610, it was only sent in small quantities and was viewed largely as a medicinal remedy. This may well have been to avoid disapproval by the Puritans who were very suspicious of the new drink!

How Did Tea Get its Name?

A nice cup of cha? Tea was first called "cha" from the Cantonese slang word for tea, ch'a. The name changed to tay or tee, when the British trading post moved from Canton to Amoy, where the word for tea is t'e. The word chai is currently used by English speakers to identify spicy teas of Indian origin.

HOW TEA BECAME FASHIONABLE IN ENGLAND

You won't be surprised to learn that the British habit of drinking tea came about with a royal seal of approval! When Charles II brought his new Portuguese wife, Catherine of Braganza, over to England in 1662, she brought with her some of her favourite tea. Tea had been well established in Portugal, as the Portuguese were the first to establish trading relations with China. The tea was part of her dowry and she introduced it to the court circle. Thus tea gained social acceptance among the aristocracy.

Ironically, even though his wife introduced tea-drinking to the English court, it was under the reign of Charles II that tea was first taxed, adding greatly to its cost. Part of the problem for the government was that tea was beginning to overtake the consumption of alcohol and the resulting loss of tax revenue was a cause of great concern.

Tea Importation and Smuggling

In the mid 1600's, there was tremendous rivalry and conflict between the English and Dutch over trading rights, routes and territories. In 1669, an English law was passed prohibiting the importation of Dutch supplied tea into the British market.

This situation led to the widespread smuggling of tea. Inevitably, smuggled tea had a distinct price advantage over legally imported tea because it avoided import duty, which was in excess of 100% of the value of the tea.

Ships from Holland brought tea to the British coast, then stayed offshore while smugglers met them and unloaded the precious cargo into small vessels. The smugglers, often local fishermen, would bring the tea inland through underground passages and hidden paths to special hiding places. Churches often proved to be favourite hiding places for their "stash"!

The Price of Tea

When it first arrived in England, tea was very much a luxury. To give you an example; in 1706, Thomas Twining was selling Gunpowder Green Tea for a price that's equivalent at today's rates of more than £160 for 100 grams (3½ ounces). As tea was such a precious commodity, it was not unusual for it to be locked away in a tea caddy.

A popular way to economise was to save the leaves from the morning brew for a second brewing later in the day. This would often be a "perk" offered to domestic staff in wealthy homes. This practise could possibly be another factor that led to tea becoming more popular than coffee, which could only be brewed once and therefore worked out to be more expensive.

Canny tea merchants, tempted to exploit customers' ignorance, would sometimes mix high quality teas with inferior ones. This process of "thinning out" could occur several times over, as corrupt retailers and middlemen increased their profits at each stage.

The Boston Tea Party

Tea played a significant role in the American War of Independence. The Tea Act of 1773, passed by the British Parliament, ordered the American colonies to pay tax on tea and this caused great resentment, leading to what became known as the Boston Tea Party. By way of protest, a group of Massachusetts colonists, disguised as Mohawks, boarded three British tea ships in Boston Harbour and hurled the tea chests overboard.

BOSTON TEA PARTY

The Growth of an Industry

In the second half of the 19th Century a major advancement in the tea trade involved the famous Clippers, which were fast sailing ships that raced across the seas, laden with tea. The clippers literally "clipped" the journey time dramatically, to an average of 4 months, thus reducing the overheads and ensuring that the tea arrived in a much fresher condition.

A Little Known Fact About Clippers

To maximise space, the Chinese stevedores, who packed the tea, used to mould the tea chests to the curve of the ship by beating them into place with wooden mallets. This also served to stabilise the ships which often had to withstand heavy gales and even monsoons. Cash prizes were offered in specially arranged races to encourage faster delivery time.

When Did the First English Advertisement for Tea Appear?

The first record is in 1657, when tea was advertised for sale at a coffee house called the Sultaness Head, by a merchant named Thomas Garway, also known and referred to as Garraway. Later that same year, Garway, advertised tea at his own London coffee house, Garway's, in Exchange Alley in the City of London, and he painted a rosy picture of the new drink. Long before the days of advertising regulations, he waxed lyrical about its benefits and according to his claims, there was hardly an ailment that this miracle leaf couldn't cure!

The Cutty Sark

One of the most famous of these clippers is the "Cutty Sark" (built in 1869), the oldest surviving tea clipper in the world and a popular tourist attraction in Greenwich, south east London. Sadly, it was the subject of an extensive fire, in May 2007. Fortunately, because it ("she"!) was undergoing a £25m restoration at the time, much of the ship had already been removed and the damage was not as irreparable as first thought. It has since been awarded some lottery money and private funding.

The Suez Canal

It was the introduction of steam ships and the opening of the Suez Canal in 1869, that ended the relatively short era (30 years) of these rather romantic ships, which are always depicted with their vast sails billowing in the wind.

Tea was a Major Factor in the Wealth of the British Empire

By 1836 the East India Company was importing 49,000,000 lbs of tea per year and the cultivation and manufacture of tea became one of the most important economic activities of the British Empire. The tea trade also spawned a wealth of secondary industries to serve the needs of the tea planters and merchants.

When Did Indian Tea Come to England and Revolutionise its Availability?

It wasn't until the late 19th century that the same East India merchants began to grow tea in India and then Ceylon, in order not to have to depend so heavily on imports from China. After much trial and error, the great English tea marketing companies were founded and production was mechanised with the Industrial Revolution, in the late 1880's. This made a huge difference to the cost of tea and made it much more available to the public in general.

CHAPTER *7*

Tea-drinking in England

THIS CHAPTER TRACES THE ORIGINS OF TEA-DRINKING in England, from its initial introduction in coffee houses, to tea gardens and into the homes of the gentry, where it eventually became central to that great British institution of afternoon tea.

COFFEE HOUSES

Ironically, it was actually in coffee houses that tea was first served and grew to such popularity in England. Coffee houses seem to have been an early forerunner to gentlemen's clubs and were places where patrons could read the newspapers and hold discussions with like-minded contemporaries. They were male-only hubs of business, social interaction and entertainment. Some housed auctions, while others sold tickets for plays and balls. Subscription libraries were first started in coffee houses and a few acted as editorial offices of newspapers or magazines, which became known as "penny universities". Some of the coffee houses became so politically active that in 1667, the government declared them to be a "…resort of idle and disaffected persons", and tried to abolish them. The gentlemen rebelled and Parliament was forced to repeal its decision.

At one time there were about 2,500 coffee houses squeezed into a 3–5 kilometre (2–3 mile) radius of central London. One of the first of these was owned by Thomas Garraway (see page 102), who in 1657, as "a merchant with an eye for a deal", introduced tea as a medicinal drink that could "make the body active and lusty"! He would often hold auctions of goods captured in the war, such as "one box of chocolates, forty six bags of snuff and one elephant's tooth".

Competition between the coffee houses was stiff and proprietors were always on the lookout for new and imaginative ideas to boost trade or capture the trade of a particular clientele. For example, Edward Lloyd, the founder of insurers Lloyds of London, opened his coffee shop in 1687. He would display a list of ships that were due to sail, along with their cargoes. This encouraged the underwriters to meet in his coffee house and arrange the insurance, and in turn, spend money.

Coffee houses were not places where women who valued their reputations would frequent. Regardless of how elegant the coffee shop was, they would still send a servant to buy tea or coffee on their behalf.

Coffee Houses Frequented by the Great and the Good

Samuel Pepys was very much the "man-about-town" and would often frequent coffee houses. He is reported to have been extremely fond of tea. On Sunday 25 September 1660, he recorded in his diary "I took a Cupp of Tee (a China drink) of which I never had drank before."

Samuel Johnson, whose reputation was established by his *Dictionary of the English Language*, was another aficionado of coffee houses. He was said to "enjoy literary conversation to amuse his evening hours". One of his companions was Joshua Reynolds, portrait painter and aesthetician.

THE LONDON TEA GARDENS

The introduction of tea gardens in the first half of the eighteenth century, brought about a change in English social life, particularly for women. As we have seen, coffee houses were very much the province of gentlemen, but the opening of the London tea gardens seems to have paved the way for women to socialise more freely. For the first time, women were permitted to enter a mixed public gathering without social criticism, provided that is, that they were accompanied by a male escort.

The tea gardens were specifically designed leisure gardens, where ladies and gentlemen were served tea outdoors, amid flowered walkways and bowling greens. They were entertained by orchestras, concerts, gambling and often fireworks at night. Hidden arbours were an obvious attraction for those in search of a secret romance. It was at just such a tea garden that Lord Nelson, who famously defeated Napoleon in the Battle of Trafalgar, was said to have met Emma, the great love of his life.

As the gardens were public, British society mixed for the first time, cutting across lines of class and birth. The tea gardens were generally open from May to September, with the exception of Sundays. The cost of entry was originally one shilling and only "known ladies of ill repute" were barred entry. The most popular of these tea gardens were Vauxhall and Ranelagh.

The Vauxhall Pleasure Gardens

The original Vauxhall Pleasure Gardens (also known as New Spring Gardens) opened in 1661 and were built close to Vauxhall Bridge, on the site now occupied by the Tate Britain. However, it wasn't until they were remodelled in 1732 that they started to attract the attention of the fashionable London set. The opening night was quite spectacular and visitors witnessed the arrival of the Prince of Wales himself, who had travelled down on a barge,

Caneletto painted this famous view of the Grand Walk (Vauxhall) in 1751.

directly from Kew Palace.

The gardens were famous for their lavish entertainment. There were illuminated fountains, balloon ascents and even, in 1827, a re-enactment of the Battle of Waterloo, involving 1,000 soldiers!

Vauxhall Gardens reached the height of their popularity in the early 1800s, with 20,000 people visiting on one night in 1826. Needless to say, with so many people walking around, the gardens were a haven for pickpockets. Every evening at 9pm, a watchman would ring a bell and shout "take care of your pockets".

BELOW *Fire balloon ascent at Vauxhall Pleasure Gardens, performed in 1802 by André Jacques Garnerin.*

These gardens were the inspiration for the creation of the Tivoli Gardens in Copenhagen and indeed, numerous other pleasure gardens around Europe. They also inspired Canaletto, who painted the famous view of the Grand Walk c. 1751 (see page 107). In fact, the term "Vauxhall" became a generic term for other pleasure gardens, including Bath's Sydney Gardens, often visited by Jane Austen. The Vauxhall Gardens opened for the last time on the night of Monday 25 July 1859.

A Walk in the Gardens With Casanova

In her book *Dr. Johnson's London*, Liza Picard tells of how one summer evening, Casanova offered a woman two guineas if she would "come and take a little walk with me in a dark alley". Apparently she took the money and ran!

Ranelagh Gardens

Ranelegh Gardens

The main rival to Vauxhall was Ranelagh Gardens (also spelt Ranelegh and Ranleigh), which were constructed in 1741 on a site previously owned by the Earl of Ranelagh. In order to create the pleasure gardens, the Earl's house and grounds were purchased by a syndicate that included the owner of the Theatre Royal, Drury Lane.

When they opened in 1742, the gardens at Ranelegh were considered more fashionable than those at Vauxhall and the entrance fee of two shillings and sixpence was more than double that of Vauxhall. However, this entry fee included tea or coffee and bread and butter (no alcohol was served!). It was considered an extremely desirable place to see and be seen and was a popular haunt of the royals.

The grounds included a canal with gondolas and flowered walkways. It is not hard to see why it was considered such a perfect place for romance and many an introduction is said to have taken place at Ranelagh – "the most convenient place for courtships of every kind — the best market we have in England". One of the major attractions of Ranelagh was the "rotunda" or dome, which was built in the rococo style and it was here that Mozart performed in 1765 when he was only nine years old.

The Rotunda in Ranelegh Gardens

In 1749, to celebrate the end of the War of Austrian Succession by the Treaty of Aix la Chapelle, King George II was persuaded to hold a jubilee masquerade. According to a description by Horace Walpole, "Everyone came in masks, the amphitheatre was illuminated and decorated with greenery and orange trees, with small lamps in each orange and below them the finest auriculas in pots…there were booths for tea and wine, gaming tables and dancing and about two thousand persons".

The site is now part of the grounds of Chelsea Hospital – home of the famous Chelsea Pensioners and also the annual Chelsea Flower Show.

AFTERNOON TEA ARRIVES

To set the scene, you need to know that we are talking about the early 1840s, shortly after the young Victoria had come to the throne as Queen of England at the age of 18, in 1837.

As a result of the new gas lighting which began in the 1830s, days started earlier and ended later. Consequently, breakfast was eaten earlier and supper was often not served until 9pm. Lunch was not usually a very substantial meal and the long gap must have created somewhat of a problem as far as "rumbling tummies" were concerned!

Victorian people tended to drink tea with their breakfast and then perhaps after dinner. In fact it was all because the lovely Anna Maria, Seventh Duchess of Bedford, was feeling a bit "peckish" in the long stretch between a light lunch and late dinner, that the habit of drinking tea mid-afternoon really began to catch on.

One particular afternoon, Anna, a very practical woman, clearly felt in need of a "pick-me up" as she had what was so aptly described as "that sinking feeling"! She sensibly decided to ask her maid to go to the kitchen and bring her a pot of tea, some bread and butter and some little cakes. This seems to have had the desired effect and she began to make a regular habit of it. Being quite a sociable soul, she soon began inviting other ladies of the court to join her in this little afternoon treat. Naturally her friends reciprocated and began issuing their own invitations to afternoon tea. Gradually, privileged members of Victorian society embraced the idea of afternoon tea and it became an essential engagement on everyone's social calendar.

The Life of Lady Anna Maria (1783–1857)

Lady Anna Maria (1783–1857)

It is worth noting that Anna Maria lived to be 74 years old, which in Victorian times was a very long life indeed! Perhaps there is a connection between the nutritional benefits she received from the extra fortification provided by her afternoon treats and her longevity. I have a very strong sympathy for Anna, as my own personal belief is very much in line with the old adage of "a little of what you fancy does you good"! Let me tell you a little more about this very charming woman, who reportedly had such an impact on English social life.

Anna was originally Lady Anna Maria Stanhope and became Marchioness of Tavistock when she married Francis Russell, Marquess of Tavistock. In 1839, Francis became Seventh Duke of Bedford making Anna his Duchess and they inherited the ancestral home of Woburn Abbey.

Queen Victoria Visits Woburn Abbey

In 1841, Queen Victoria and Prince Albert spent the night at Woburn Abbey and the Queen wrote in her diary, "…in the bedroom and my dressing room there are some very fine pictures: in the former hangs one of Lord Russell's trial by Hayter, one by Wilkie, a Landseer, a beautiful St John by Hayter with his portrait of Lord John and a very fine Eastlake." With the exception of the Wilkie and Eastlake, these paintings remain in the Woburn collection. Queen Victoria herself presented Anna Maria with some etchings drawn by her and Prince Albert, and these are now hung in the same bedroom in which she stayed.

Woburn Abbey

Woburn Abbey has been the home of the Dukes of Bedford for nearly 400 years and is now occupied by the Fifteenth Duke and his family. The house is set in 1,214 hectares (3,000 acres) of parkland and includes an award-winning safari park. It is only about an hour's drive from London and is well worth a visit.

One of the most prestigious roles within the British royal household is that of a lady-in-waiting to the queen. Anna was honoured to be given the position of Lady-of-the-bedchamber to Queen Victoria and, as one of her many privileges, she had an apartment in Buckingham Palace and her own personal lady's maid.

The role of a lady-in-waiting tends to evolve according to the wishes of the queen, but the candidates are always chosen from high-ranking members of the aristocracy (noble women). One of Anna's main duties would have been to keep company with the young Queen and to assist her in entertaining visiting dignitaries to the court. Anna held the position from 1837–1841 and, after becoming Duchess of Bedford in 1839, she would have divided her time between Woburn Abbey and Buckingham Palace.

TEA GOWNS

This delightful creation entered the fashion scene in the 1870s, at a time when both day and evening wear fitted very closely to the body. By contrast, the typical tea gown hung loosely from the shoulders, often with a draped back and bodice shaped with pleating, shirring or smocking.

When you think of the way Afternoon Tea emerged; as an intimate invitation from the Duchess of Bedford to her close friends to join her in her private salon for tea, the way in which the structure of the tea gown itself developed, over time, makes complete sense.

The first tea gowns were only slightly dressier than "morning robes" but as time progressed, they gradually became more elaborate and evolved into highly desirable and fashionable afternoon garments.

There were in fact two catergories of tea gown: robe d'interieur and robe d'exterieur. The "robe d'interieur" was worn in the home by the wealthy hostess who invited her close friends and family to join her for afternoon tea "at home". They would also have been packed in the suitcases of visiting friends who were invited by the hostess to stay overnight or for weekend house parties, which were very popular at this time. These gowns tended to be far less formal in terms of structure than those worn outside of the home ("robe d'exterieur") by invited guests.

However, although less formal in structure than those worn for outer wear, there were no bounds to the lavishness of a "robe d'interieur": (Please see accompanying picture.) The femininity of these tea gowns, with their luxurious trimmings and loose styling, made them

a very popular edition to the fashionable wardrobe of their privileged wearers. These highly social ladies with time on their hands were in some ways an early equivalent of modern day "ladies who lunch"!

The term "robe d'exterieur", was used to describe the much more practical, structured tea gowns which were worn outside of the home, by ladies who were invited to tea but were not actually staying with the hostess.

As well as being worn for afternoon tea, tea gowns were

Tea for Two

These rather seductive gowns, with their relative ease of fastening, were also associated with more personal "at home" invitations from the hostess!

It was not unknown for an afternoon invitation to be issued to a favoured gentleman caller, on the understanding that the lady would be "at home" to nobody but him. Discreet servants would smooth the way for an undisturbed visit and the lady's husband would more than likely be detained from home by similar pursuits of his own.

"robe d'interieur"
This lovely example of a tea gown was designed c. 1900 by the French designer Rouff.

also considered appropriate wear for informal dinners in the home.

Although most tea gowns would have been worn over corsets, a significant factor was that some of them had un-boned bodices. This allowed for greater freedom of movement (and, no doubt, more room for the wearer to indulge in tasty teatime treats!) In this respect, they contributed to the trend towards a more casual style of dressing and reflected aspects of a movement towards a new freedom for women.

By Invitation Only

Afternoon tea created a market for all sorts of fashion accessories associated with the ritual. Not being able to simply pick up the phone and invite their friends over, hostesses had to send out handwritten invitations, which could be elegantly simple or elaborately decorative.

WHEN DID AFTERNOON TEA FIRST "GO PUBLIC"?

Initially, afternoon tea was enjoyed almost exclusively by the upper classes in their own homes and it didn't really "go public" until 1884. The first "proper" tearoom in Britain was opened in London in the London Bridge area. It was known as the ABC (Aerated Bread Company) tearoom.

It was the particularly imaginative manageress of the ABC bakery who persuaded the owners of the company to allow her to serve afternoon tea on the premises. Gradually, ABC tearooms opened up all over the country and were soon followed by other popular chains such as Kardomah, the Express Dairy and the J. Lyons sumptuous Corner Houses. The first Lyons Corner House had red silk on the walls, gas chandeliers, red plush chairs

Tea Break

The introduction of cheaper tea in the late 1880s was timely for the workers in the newly-created factories. During their breaks, they welcomed the comfort offered by a hot mug of tea, that was usually fortified with milk and sugar. The caffeine obviously provided them with a much needed lift and the warmth of the drink served to compensate for the lack of a hot meal.

The Ritz Hotel, London

and waitresses dressed in elegant floor-length uniforms. Most department stores began to serve afternoon tea and Whiteleys in Bayswater even introduced a female orchestra to add to the atmosphere. The Ritz Hotel, London, was the first establishment to permit unescorted ladies to enter to enjoy afternoon tea. Tearooms flourished, but due to the effects of rationing and the general austerity that followed the Second World War, they gradually dwindled. Today, sadly, there are relatively few tearooms in major towns, but I'm happy to say that delicious afternoon teas are still very much available in luxury hotels, department stores and country villages.

TEA DANCES "AT HOME"

It was not uncommon for wealthy members of Victorian society to entertain their friends with tea dances at home. If there wasn't a separate room available, furniture would be pushed aside to create space. The usual afternoon tea fare would be served but the dancing would often carry on until supper time, when guests would be refreshed with drinks such as lemonade and fruit punch. These occasions were demure and elegant, but at last offered a viable event at which the gentlemen could join the ladies.

PUBLIC TEA DANCES

It was a natural progression from the tea gardens and "at home" tea dances that the idea of the public tea dance developed and reached the height of popularity with the arrival of the tango from Argentina in 1910. When the tango first arrived, it seems to have literally taken London by storm! It was first performed on stage in a play called "The Sunshine Girl", performed at the Gaiety Theatre and it instantly became a craze. Everybody wanted to learn the tango and classes sprung up all over the country. However, as you can imagine, this exotic and somewhat risqué dance was much modified in order not to shock the Victorians.

After the disruption of the First World War, tea dances never really recovered their popularity, although they remained highly fashionable. With the advent of the Second World War, they gradually disappeared from the social scene, with two notable exceptions – namely the Waldorf and the Savoy hotels. The Waldorf Hotel in London (now a Hilton hotel) was the last of the great London hotels to finally give up this delightful institution in 2004. The Savoy Hotel in London stopped holding them just one year earlier in 2003.

CHAPTER 8

Tracing the History of the Teapot

HERE'S A SUBJECT THAT DEFINITELY DESERVES a whole chapter in its own right – the trusty teapot! The use of teapots has evolved over centuries, reflecting the evolution of the production and consumption of tea. The invention of the tea bag has certainly made quite an impact on the way in which tea is served. It is now all too easy to make tea directly in a mug or cup using a tea bag. In fact, in modern Britain, many people don't use teapots at all except on special occasions. The use of a teapot transforms the experience of serving tea but understandably, when people are in a hurry, they often prefer to use tea bags. There's a time and a place for the bag in a cup or a mug but there is still, most definitely, a time and a place for the teapot. Here, I'm going to take you on a whirlwind trip through its history.

Who Invented the Teapot?

Believe it or not, there isn't a definite answer to this question. The earliest pottery pot that has the shape of today's teapot can be dated to seventh–eighth-century China during the Tang Dynasty (618–917). It is thought likely that this unglazed pot was originally intended to serve wine. However, it seems reasonable to assume that, over time, these same wine pourers were used as teapots. Similarly, pots originally designed for coffee in Europe, were initially interchangeable and used for tea and hot chocolate.

Chinese Teapots

One historical viewpoint is that, initially, the Chinese did not use teapots to make their tea, but bowls. One explanation for this could be because of the way in which tea was produced in eighth-century China. Rather than being used in leaf form, the dried leaves were ground into a powder, mixed with salt and then formed into cakes. These cakes were placed in bowls of hot water and they dissolved, making a thick liquid. Over the years, the

117
~

The Yixing teapot

process altered, and the powder was left in its loose form. It was then made by mixing it in a bowl with boiling water. This was then whisked into a frothy mixture. This way of making tea (Matcha) was introduced into Japan in the ninth century. Up until the fifteenth century, tea was drunk in both of these countries primarily as a medicinal remedy. It was only after this time that it was drunk for ceremonial purposes.

According to other historical sources, the Chinese brewed tea in what was known as a "medicine pot" or kettle. The tea was placed in a special clay pot that was filled up with water and then simmered and reduced. The tea would be drunk directly from the spout, which served as a filter.

Leaf infusion or brewing tea in the way that we are now all familiar with, began in China at the beginning of the Ming Dynasty (1368–1644), making this period the most probable date of birth for the teapot. Early examples of the famous Yixing teapots date from this period and the general thinking is that these pots were made as smaller versions of the traditional Chinese medicine pots. The tea was brewed in the Yixing teapot and also drunk from it as well.

The Japanese Tetsubin Teapot

Some of the most beautiful and carefully crafted teapots in the world are the Tetsubin teapots of Japan. Like the Yixing teapots in China, they became popular some time in the late seventeenth century when Sencha (whole leaf

tea) became more widespread. Tetsubin pots were originally used as kettles, but as tea-drinking became more commonplace, more affordable pots than those imported from China were needed, so the Tetsubin was used as a teapot.

European Teapots

It is highly likely that the design of early Chinese pieces influenced the first European teapots. However, while the design of many of the early pots was often innovative, the quality of the pots was poor. At this point in time, Europe still lagged way behind China in terms of the necessary technology to manufacture quality porcelain.

As Europe became industrialised, a new middle class was born, keen to spend their disposable income on fashionable items for the home. In England, this included exquisite china and linen needed to host the new and fashionable ritual of afternoon tea. Initially, they bought teaware directly from China until Josiah Spode perfected the formula for fine bone china. This obviously opened the door for other manufacturers in the industry.

Teapot manufacture went from the functional, to the beautiful, to the somewhat fantastical. Teapot design followed major artistic and design trends and the same is still true today.

A Word (or Two!) About Infusers

I'm going to finish this chapter on a very practical note. Students often ask me about infusers and infuser teapots, so I thought it might be helpful to give you as much information about them as possible, so that you can make up your own mind. The point of infusers is that they help avoid the problem of over-brewed tea, which can, on occasion, become bitter.

Whether you are using a separate infuser, a filter or a teapot with a built-in infuser, the principle is the same – the infuser needs to be large enough to allow the tea leaves sufficient room to move and expand, which is essential for achieving maximum extraction of flavour.

Infuser Teapots

There are many different types of infuser teapot on the market. All of the pots work equally well, so it really comes down to personal choice – do you prefer to remove an infuser,

press on a plunger or twist a lid?

Some teapots contain infusers that can be lifted out of the pot when the tea has finished infusing, preventing the tea from becoming over-steeped and bitter. The patented, traditionally shaped Chatsford teapot is an excellent example of this type of pot and is made from either bone china or earthenware.

The Bodum® teapot that I use works a little differently; it contains a plunger. When you decide that the tea has infused for long enough, you depress the plunger, separating the leaves from the hot water.

Another example, the Finum Tea Control, has a patented insert, allowing you to twist the lid of the teapot to separate the leaves from the water.

The advantage of having teapots with built-in infusers, is that there is no risk of mess caused by a dripping infuser as it is removed from the pot.

Infusers and Filters

If you already have, or prefer to use, a traditional teapot, there are both disposable and reusable infusers/filters that can be used with it to make a perfect pot of tea.

Reusable infusers come in a variety of shapes, sizes and materials. When choosing, remember to select one that allows maximum contact between the leaves and the water. Mesh infusers, whether made of metal or plastic, are preferable to the solid metal infusers that only have a few holes perforated in them. The solid metal ones often come in various cute shapes like teapots, houses or teddy bears, but try to overlook the 'cute factor' when selecting a good infuser. Remember that size is very much an issue too; the infuser should be large enough to allow the tea leaves to expand fully.

If you don't want the mess of dumping out tea leaves and rinsing an infuser, then disposable tea filters are a very practical alternative. An example is the T-sac filter. The principle of using a filter is exactly the same as an infuser, except that when infusion is complete, the filter can be disposed of like a tea bag. They are made of unbleached paper and are gusseted at the bottom to allow room for the leaves to expand. They generally come in three different sizes to accommodate mugs and small and large teapots

TO SUM UP

Having said all this, I certainly don't remember my mother or her friends ever using infusers and their tea was none the worse for it! I find that if you are using good quality fresh tea and you pour it out after the appropriate infusion time (usually 3–5 minutes) you can survive perfectly well without an infuser. After the first pouring, you can refresh the remainder with very hot water, ready for second cups.

I am delighted to see that Edward Bramah, the curator of The Bramah Museum of Tea and Coffee near London Bridge, agrees with me on this point. I recently visited his excellent museum and had the loveliest pot of tea and tasty sandwich. They also serve delicious scones with clotted cream and I highly recommend a visit to this very special and unique London "treasure"! It is a real "find" and I am delighted to be able to recommend it so unreservedly.

Sadly, since writing this, Edward Bramah passed away in February 2008. I do hope the museum continues to flourish.

CHAPTER 9

Tea and Health

Drinking a daily cup of tea
will surely starve the apothecary.
CHINESE PROVERB

THE CHINESE HAVE CLAIMED FOR OVER 5,000 YEARS that tea is good for health in a variety of ways. In particular, it is thought to enhance the flow of "chi energy" throughout the body and this quote by a Chinese poet sums it up beautifully:

The first cup moistens my lips and throat,
The second banishes my loneliness,
The third expells the dullness of my mind
Sharpening inspiration gained from all the books I've read,
The fourth raises a light perspiration – all the wrongs of life pass out through my pores,
The fifth cup cleanses every atom of my being,
The sixth calls me to the realms of the immortals,
The seventh... ah, but I can take no more!
I only feel the breath of the cool wind that raises in my sleeves,
Where is Elysium?
Let me ride on this sweet breeze and waft away winter.
LU TUNG

It is said to be because of its effect on "chi energy", that tea is the chosen drink for those involved in practices based on chi, such as qi gong, tai chi and aikido.

It has been claimed that an estimated 165,000,000 cups of tea are drunk every day in the UK. This is a pretty spectacular statistic, so it is certainly worth taking a peek at what it is reputed to do for our health!

WHAT CLAIMS HAVE BEEN MADE ABOUT TEA OVER THE YEARS?

We know that as far as health was concerned, the arrival of tea in Britain in the seventeenth century was extremely welcome and timely. At that time most water was unfit to drink unless boiled, so the addition of tea made it much more appealing. Prior to the introduction of tea, it was commonplace to drink ale at breakfast time, so tea offered a very welcome alternative!

In 1667, tea merchant Thomas Garraway advertised tea as "wholesome, preserving perfect health until extreme old age, good for clearing the sight… gripping of the guts, cold, dropsies, scurveys…"

In the late seventeenth century, the East India Company advertised tea as "a panacea for apoplexy, catarrh, colic, consumption, drowsiness, epilepsy, gallstones, lethargy, migraine, paralysis and vertigo".

Une Tasse de Thé Pour la Santé

Cardinal Mazarin (1602–1661) the regent in France in Louis XIV's early reign claimed that it helped to ease his gout.
King Louis XIV of France (1638–1715) drank tea to prevent vertigo and the "vapours".

In 1818, a booklet entitled the *The Lady and Gentleman's Tea Table*, stated that "if taken regularly twice a day, and in large quantities, tea is attended with bad consequences', but it gave encouraging remarks, stating that "its use after dinner, or eating, is of great service in assisting digestion, and preventing uneasiness which attends a full, weakly stomach".

Following the passing of the 1870 Education Act and the resulting universal provision of state elementary education, strenuous efforts were made to include instruction in diet, nutrition and household management in the curriculum. Accordingly, a school textbook was commissioned by the School Board for London and included an appendix for teachers with lesson plans, recipes and so on. So it came about, that in 1876, W.B. Tegetmeier wrote in *The Scholars' Handbook of Household Management and Cookery*, that tea "pleasantly excites the nervous system, increases respiration, and the action of the skin, and tends to quicken digestion. It has a decidedly soothing effect upon the action of the heart, and hence is often advantageously employed in cases of palpitation and headache."

However, not everybody was so quick to celebrate the properties of tea. Writer of books on domestic economy for the working man, William Cobbett wrote letters to newspapers decrying the increasing popularity of tea drinking and the fact that it had taken the place of ale as the nation's drink of choice. He wrote, "It is notorious that tea has no useful strength in it; and that it contains nothing nutritious; that it, besides being good for nothing, has badness in it, because it is well-known to produce want of sleep in many cases, and in all cases, to shake and weaken the nerves." He also said, "I view the tea drinking as a destroyer of health, an enfeebler of the frame, an engenderer of effeminacy and laziness, a debaucher of youth and a maker of misery for old age."

During the twentieth century, very few negative things have been said about tea. Essentially, modern research into the health benefits of tea has given credence to many old wives' tales and ancient theories. Research has proved that our daily "cuppa" offers all sorts of benefits. The UK Tea Council today states that, "All types of tea contain flavonoids; antioxidant compounds that form part of a healthy diet. These flavonoids can help protect our bodies against life-threatening illnesses such as cancer and heart disease. The average daily intake of three or four cups of tea can provide roughly the same amount of antioxidants as eating eight apples."

Talk About Tannins and Polyphenols

Quite a lot of confusion seems to have arisen over the issue of tannin in tea and I must admit that the thought of it bearing any resemblance to something that turns animal hide into leather has never held much attraction for me! So, I am delighted to report that this notion has arisen over a complete misinterpretation of scientific terminology and the term now used, to avoid confusion, is polyphenols (flavonoids). So we can all relax – tea does not contain tannins or tannic acid! Essentially polyphenols are powerful antioxidants and appear to be responsible for many of the health-boosting qualities of tea.

Current research suggests that the regular consumption of tea may help to:

- boost the immune system by increasing the number of white blood cells in the body.
- lower LDL cholesterol.
- reduce the risk of cardiovascular diseases, such as strokes and heart attacks.
- reduce the risk of certain cancers by lowering the rate of cell replication.
- repair cell damage.
- reduce the undesirable bacteria and increase beneficial bacteria in the stomach.
- digest fats.
- reduce tooth decay and strengthen tooth enamel.
- increase concentration and alertness.
- provide essential minerals e.g. manganese, zinc, potassium and magnesium.
- slow the ageing process.

Fluid Intake

We are constantly reminded by health professionals to drink more water to keep our bodies hydrated, so does tea count?

According to the British Dietetic Association, because it is a mild diuretic, a cup of tea is only equivalent to about half a cup of water.

Can Black Tea Relieve Stress?

According to a recent study commissioned by University College London, there is scientific evidence to prove that black tea aids stress relief. Results showed that the levels of cortisol (the stress hormone) in tea-drinking study participants, decreased by an average of 47 per cent compared with just 27 per cent in the control group that were given a placebo. In response to these findings, the UK Tea Council's William Gorman says, "This new research adds to the evidence that drinking tea is good for you. Not only does tea hydrate and offer some protection against heart disease and some cancers, it's now proven to de-stress too. It's great to know that a cuppa, one of life's great comforts, can be enjoyed not just for the taste, but also for its health benefits."

> ## Fresh is Best
>
> What is very clear is that to gain the maximum benefits it is essential to drink fresh tea that has been stored correctly.

Green Versus Black

Studies on both green and black tea suggest that the regular drinking of either may help lower the incidence of mortality from major chronic diseases. There has even been a suggestion from scientists in California (from the health care organisation, Kaiser Permanente) that drinking small amounts of tea can help with female fertility. Compounds in both green and black teas are thought to have a positive impact, but debate continues as to which kind of tea is healthiest.

Caffeine

Many different factors determine the way that individuals are affected by caffeine and it is important to be aware of your own tolerance level. The way in which we are affected by caffeine is largely due to our metabolism, exposure and habit. Some people have no trouble sleeping after a cup of tea or coffee, whereas to those who are highly sensitive to it, caffeine can cause insomnia. While the positive stimulant effect of caffeine can be uplifting and mood enhancing (at the right time of day!), too much can have quite the opposite effect. Gradual withdrawal is thought to be the most effective way of dealing with caffeine addiction.

How Much Caffeine is it Safe to Drink ?

According to the UK Tea Council, (www.tea.co.uk) up to 300 milligrams per day is generally considered to be an acceptable amount of caffeine for the average adult. However, it's not just a matter of calculating how many cups of tea or coffee you can have in a day; you need to take into account the caffeine that you take in from other sources. For example: cola drinks and some energy drinks can be quite high in caffeine; medication (e.g. some headache preparations) also contain caffeine; chocolate is another source, so tea-drinking chocaholics beware! It is certainly worth keeping an eye on your daily caffeine level and making sure that you don't have more than the equivalent of six cups of tea OR four cups of coffee if you want to stay healthy and relaxed. NB: Cups are not the same as mugs! See below for guidelines.

Because children metabolise at a faster rate than adults, it is generally considered wise to restrict their intake of caffeine.

How Much Caffeine is there in a Regular Cup of Tea?

In general, black tea contains the most caffeine, while oolong, green and white tea contain progressively less, in that order.

Needless to say, actual levels are dependent on specific teas and the strength of the infusion. As a guide, an average cup (190 millilitres/6½ fluid ounces) of regular black tea contains about 45 milligrams of caffeine, which is about a third less than the same sized cup of instant coffee, which contains 70 milligrams.

Final Diagnosis

Despite all these claims in praise of tea, you won't need me to remind you that tea is not a proven magical shortcut to health and beauty but is considered to be a complimentary addition to a healthy, balanced diet and lifestyle.

Although the health benefits of tea are not yet fully proven, the results of modern scientific research and studies are very positive, indicating that there may well be some truth in what the Chinese people have believed for over 5,000 years.

> NOTE:
> All content is provided for general information only, and should not be treated as a substitute for the medical advice of your own doctor or any other health care professional. Always consult your own GP if you're in any way concerned about your health.

CHAPTER 10
Tea Quotations

AS WE HAVE SEEN, THE SUBJECT OF TEA provokes strong and passionate views, and sometimes quite extraordinary claims by an interesting cross-section of the glitterati. I never cease to be surprised by the number of literary works, speeches and even stand-up comedians that mention tea. It seems that everyone wants to have their say!

THE GREAT CURE-ALL AND RESCUER FROM ALL ILLS

If you are cold, tea will warm you;
If you are too heated, it will cool you;
If you are depressed, it will cheer you;
If you are excited, it will calm you.
WILLIAM GLADSTONE
(1809–1898; *four-times prime minister of UK*)

There is no trouble so great
or grave that cannot be much
diminished by a nice cup of tea.
BERNARD-PAUL HEROUX
(1900s *Baroque philosopher*)

Drinking a daily cup of tea will surely
starve the apothecary.
CHINESE PROVERB

Tea's proper use is to amuse the idle, and relax the studious, and dilute the full meals of those who cannot use exercise, and will not use abstinence.
SAMUEL JOHNSON
(1709–1784; *poet, essayist, biographer and lexicographer*)

Tea is drunk to forget the din of the world.
T'IEN YIHENG
(*Chinese philosopher and tea enthusiast*)

Tea does our fancy aid,
Repress those vapours which the head invade
And keeps that palace of the soul serene.
EDMUND WALLER
(1606–1687; *English poet and politician*)

Tea is a cup of life.
AUTHOR UNKNOWN

THE GREAT BRITISH MORALE BOOSTER AND UNIFIER

The national addiction of tea-drinking has long been recognised as a common bond by the British people. Whenever there is any kind of trauma in a British household, whether it be physical or emotional, somebody is bound to suggest that the kettle is put on for "a nice cup of tea". It has come to be seen as a panacea for all ills. It has even been reputed to have helped unite the nation in times of peril:

During the Second World War, A. A. Thompson wrote, "they talk about Hitler's secret weapon, but what about England's secret weapon? Tea. That's what keeps us going to carry us through… the Army, the Navy, the Women's Institute – what keeps 'em together is tea!"

TEA AND SOCIO-POLITICS

In "Cottage Economy", William Cobbett wrote that he was infuriated by the fact that the average labourer spent something approaching a third of his earnings on tea, and denounced the beverage as a wicked waste of time and money. Furthermore, he complained, "The tea drinking has done a great deal in bringing this nation into the state of misery in which it now is, it must be evident to every one that the practice of tea drinking must render the frame feeble, and unfit to encounter hard labour or severe weather, while… it deducts from the means of replenishing the belly and covering the back. Hence succeeds a softness, an effeminacy, a seeking for the fireside, a lurking in the bed, and, in short, all the characteristics of idleness. The progress of this famous plant has been something like the progess of truth; suspected at first, though very palatable to those who had courage to taste it; resisted as it encroached; abused as its popularity seemed to spread; and establishing its triumph at last, in cheering the whole land from the palace to the cottage, only by the slow and resistless efforts of time and its own virtues."

AESTHETICISM, PHILOSOPHY AND INSPIRATION

In his famous book *The Book of Tea*, written in 1906, Kazuko Okakura wrote, "Philosophy of tea is not mere aestheticism in the ordinary acceptance of the term, for it expresses conjointly with ethics and religion our whole point of view about man and nature."

He also wrote, "There is a subtle charm in the taste of tea which makes it irresistible and capable of idealisation… It has not the arrogance of wine, the self-consciousness of coffee, nor the simpering innocence of cocoa."

If a man has no tea in him, he is incapable of understanding truth and beauty.
JAPANESE PROVERB

Tea tempers the spirit and harmonizes the mind; dispels lassitude and relieves fatigue, awakens thought and prevents drowsiness.
Its goodness is a decision for the mouth to make.
LU YU
(733–804; *Sage of Tea*)

There is a great deal of poetry and fine sentiment in a cup of tea.
Letters and Social Aims –
RALPH WALDO EMERSON
(1803–1882; *essayist and poet*)

The subject is happiness, and I imagine a way of life – we sip tea and talk.
These are my daydreams.
MOSHE DAYAN (1915–1981; *Israeli military leader and politician*)

Each cup of tea represents an imaginary voyage.
CATHERINE DOUZEL

TEA AND CHEERFULNESS

Come, let us have some tea and continue to talk about happy things.
The Chosen – CHAIM POTOK
(1929–2002; *author and rabbi*)

The mere chink of cups and saucers tunes the mind to happy repose.
The Private Papers of Henry Ryecroft –
GEORGE GISSING
(1857–1903; *novelist*)

Yet let's be merry; we'll have tea and toast;
Custards for supper, and an endless host
Of syllabubs and jellies and mince-pies,
And other such lady-like luxuries, –
Letter to Maria Gisborne –
PERCY BYSSHE SHELLEY
(1792–1822; *poet*)

Let each and all then grateful be… and hail a welcome guest in tea.
SAMUEL PEPYS
(1633–1703; *diarist*)

TEA AND COSINESS

A wonderful picture of warmth, cosiness and homely atmosphere is conjured up in the following passages.

Now stir the fire, and close
the shutters fast,
Let fall the curtains, wheel the sofa round,
And, while the bubbling
and loud-hissing urn
Throws up a steamy column, and the cups,
That cheer but not inebriate, wait on each,
So let us welcome peaceful ev'ning in.
The Task – WILLIAM COWPER
(1731–1800; *writer and composer of hymns*)

The virtues and comfort of ritual and predictability are beautifully expressed in this extract from novelist
P. G. WODEHOUSE'S short story
Jeeves in the Springtime...
"He put the good old cup of tea softly on the table by my bed, and I took a refreshing sip. Just right, as usual. Not too hot, not too sweet, not to weak… not too much milk and not a drop spilled in the saucer… He always floats in with the cup exactly two minutes after I come to life."
He also said, "The cup of tea on arrival at a country house is a thing which, as a rule, I particularly enjoy. I like the crackling logs, the shaded lights, the scent of buttered toast, the general atmosphere of leisured cosiness."

When the world is all at odds
And the mind is all at sea
Then cease the useless tedium
And brew a cup of tea.
There is magic in its fragrance,
There is solace in its taste;
And the laden moments vanish somehow
into space.
And the world becomes a lovely thing!
There's beauty as you'll see;
All because you briefly stopped
To brew a cup of tea.
AUTHOR UNKNOWN

I am so fond of tea that I could write a whole dissertation on its virtues. It comforts and enlivens without the risks attendant on spirituous liquors. Gentle herb!
Let the florid grape yield to thee.
Thy soft influence is a more safe inspirer of social joy.
JAMES BOSWELL
(1740–1795; *lawyer, diarist and author*)

Strange how a teapot can represent at the
same time the comforts
of solitude and the pleasures of company.
AUTHOR UNKNOWN

Tea should be taken in solitude.
C. S. LEWIS
(1898–1963; *author*)

Surely everyone is aware of the divine
pleasures which attend a wintry fireside:
candles at four o'clock, warm hearth rugs,
tea, a fair tea-maker, shutters closed,
curtains flowing in ample draperies to the
floor, whilst the wind and rain are raging
audibly without.
THOMAS DE QUINCEY
(1785–1859; *author*)

Cook, Cook, drink your tea,
But save some in the pot for me.
We'll watch the tea leaves in our cup,
When our drink is all sipped up.
Happiness or fortune great,
What will our future be?
Afternoon Tea at Pittock Mansion
– R. Z. BERRY

AFTERNOON TEA

My copper kettle
whistles merrily
and signals that
it is time for tea.

The fine china cups
are filled with the brew.
There's lemon and sugar
and sweet cream, too.

But, best of all
there's friendship, between you and me.
As we lovingly share
our afternoon tea.
MARIANNA AROLIN

The tea party is a spa for the soul. You
leave your cares and work behind. Busy
people forget their business. Your stress
melts away, your senses awaken.
ALEXANDRA STODDARD (*author, interior
designer and speaker*)

Steam rises from a cup of tea and we are
wrapped in history, inhaling ancient times
and lands, comfort of ages in our hands.
FAITH GREENBOWL

Another novelty is the tea-party, an extraordinary meal in that, being offered to persons that have already dined well, it supposes neither appetite nor thirst, and has no object but distraction, no basis but delicate enjoyment.

The Physiology of Taste –
JEAN-ANTHELME BRILLAT-SAVARIN
(1755–1826;
famous French epicure and gastronome)

TIME FOR TEA

My hour for tea is half-past five, and my buttered toast waits for nobody.
WILKIE COLLINS
(1824–1889; *novelist and playwright*)

Stands the Church clock at ten to three?
And is there honey still for tea?
The Old Vicarage, Grantchester –
RUPERT BROOKE
(1887–1915; *poet*)

I know now why Franz Schubert
Never finished his unfinished symphony
He would have written more
but the clock struck four
And everything stopped for tea.
Everything Stops for Tea – JOHN BALDRY
(1941–2005; *singer*)

IN PRAISE OF TEA

Tea was certainly the favoured drink of great wit and writer Dr Samuel Johnson (1709–1784) who famously wrote *A Dictionary of the English Language*. He confessed himself, 'a hardened and shameless tea-drinker, who has for twenty years diluted his meals with this fascinating plant; whose kettle has scarcely time to cool; who with tea amuses the evening, with tea solaces the midnight, and with tea welcomes the morning.'

As his biographer James Boswell put it, "I suppose no other person ever enjoyed with more relish the infusion of that fragrant leaf than did Johnson." In a piece of verse addressed to his wife, the "good doctor" acknowledged his enormous capacity for drinking tea:

And now I pray thee,
Hetty dear
That thou will give
To me,
With cream and sugar
Soften'd well
Another cup of tea.
But hear, alas!

This mournful truth,
Nor hear it
with a frown
Thou canst not make
The tea so fast
As I can gulp it down.

Dr Johnson was not the only one who couldn't get enough of this magical brew…

Drink your tea slowly and reverently, as if it is the axis on which the world earth revolves – slowly, evenly, without rushing toward the future.
THICH NHAT HAHN
(*Vietnamese teacher, author and peace activist*)

Where there's tea there's hope.
SIR ARTHUR WING PINERO
(1855–1934; *dramatist*)

You can never get a cup of tea large enough or a book long enough to suit me.
C. S. LEWIS (1898–1963; *author*)

The spirit of the tea beverage is one of peace, comfort and refinement.
ARTHUR GRAY

"Wouldn't it be dreadful to live in a country where they didn't serve tea?" exclaimed NOEL COWARD. The "master" was just one of the many writers who have poured more praise on tea than on any other beverage apart from wine.

Better to be deprived of food for three days than of tea for one.
CHINESE PROVERB

Let each and all then grateful be… and hail a welcome guest in tea.
SAMUEL PEPYS (1633–1703; *diarist*)

Thank God for tea! What would the world do without tea? How did it exist? I am glad I was not born before tea.
Lady Holland's Memoir – SYDNEY SMITH
(1771–1845; *writer*)

LOVE AND PASSION

The best quality tea must have creases
like the leathern boot of Tartar horsemen,
curl like the dewlap of a mighty bullock,
unfold like a mist rising out of a ravine,
gleam like a lake touched by a zephyr,
and be wet and soft like a fine earth
newly swept by rain.
LU YU (733–804; *Sage of Tea*)

Tea! Thou soft, thou sober, sage, and
venerable liquid, thou innocent pretence
for bringing the wicked of both sexes
together in a morning; thou female
tongue-running, smile-smoothing,
heart-opening, wink-tipping cordial, to
whose glorious insipidity I owe the
happiest moment of my life, let me fall
prostrate thus, and… adore thee.
The Lady's Last Stake –
COLLEY CIBBER (1671–1757;
playwright, actor and poet)

Picture you upon my knee,
Just tea for two and two for tea.
Tea for Two Lyrics by IRVING CAESAR
(1895–1996; *lyricist and composer*)
and OTTO HARBACH
(1873–1963; *lyricist and librettist*)

Ecstasy is a glass full of tea
and a piece of sugar in the mouth.
ALEKSANDR PUSHKIN
(1799–1837; *author*)

Seen on a billboard outside a tea-shop in
northern Copenhagen,
"Kissing is like drinking tea with a tea
strainer, you can never get enough".

Great love affairs
start with Champagne and
end with tisane.
HONORÉ DE BALZAC
(1799–1850;
novelist and playwright)

Love and scandal
are the best sweeteners of tea.
HENRY FIELDING
(1707–1754;
novelist and dramatist)

COMIC AND WHIMSICAL QUOTES

We had a kettle; we let it leak:
Our not repairing made it worse.
We haven't had any tea for a week…
The bottom is out of the Universe.
Natural Theology – RUDYARD KIPLING
(1865–1936, *author and poet*)

⁀

LADY ASTOR (*infuriated*): Mr. Churchill, if
I were your wife, I'd put poison in your
tea. CHURCHILL: Madam, were I your
husband, I would surely drink it.
Exchange between LADY ASTOR and
WINSTON CHURCHILL, Houses of
Parliament

⁀

Tea to the English is really like a picnic
indoors.
ALICE WALKER (*Author*)

⁀

I'd rather have a cup of tea than go to bed
with someone – any day.
BOY GEORGE (*Singer and songwriter*)

The British have an umbilical cord
which has never been cut and
through which tea flows constantly.
It is curious to watch them in times of
sudden horror, tragedy or disaster.
The pulse stops apparently, and nothing
can be done, and no move made, until
"a nice cup of tea" is quickly made.
There is no question that it brings
solace and does steady the mind.
What a pity all countries are not
so tea-conscious. World-peace
conferences would run more
smoothly if "a nice cup of tea",
or indeed, a samovar were
available at the proper time
MARLENE DIETRICH
(1901–1992; *actress and singer*)

⁀

A Proper Tea is much nicer than a
very nearly tea, which is one
you forget about afterwards.
Pooh's Little Instruction Book
– A. A. MILNE
(1882–1956)

"It has never occurred to Mr. Winterbourne to offer me any tea," she said, with her little tormenting manner. "I have offered you advice," Winterbourne rejoined. "I prefer weak tea!"
Daisy Miller – HENRY JAMES
(1843–1916; *author*)

❧

Tea time – we now go back to the game of golf, because if you're playing in a competition, your captain will say to you: "Your tee time is 9.30 tomorrow", as opposed to Chinese dentists which would be: "tooth hurty" (2.30).

❧

Look here, Steward, if this is coffee, I want tea; but if this is tea, then I wish for coffee. CARTOON CAPTION, ***Punch***

❧

Our trouble is that we drink too much tea. I see in this the slow revenge of the Orient, which has diverted the Yellow River down our throats.
J. B. PRIESTLEY Quoted in ***The Observer***
(1894–1984; *writer and broadcaster*)

❧

Women are like tea bags.
We don't know our true strength until we are in hot water!
Attributed to both NANCY REAGAN and
ELEANOR ROOSEVELT

❧

"Unless the water boiling be, vain the attempt to make the tea".
KARL FAST'S GRANDMOTHER!

❧

Tea time, we now go back to the game of golf. Because if you're playing in a competition, and your captain will say to you, your tee time is 9.30 tomorrow, as opposed to Chinese dentists which would be tooth hurty, 2.30.
RICHARD (STINKER) MURDOCH
(1907–1990; *comedy performer*)

❧

Tis pity wine should be so deleterious, for tea and coffee leave us much more serious.
LORD BYRON (1788–1824; *poet*)

❧

Old maids sweeten their tea with scandal.
JOSH BILLINGS
(1818–1885; *humourist*)

❧

Alison began to cry. Mum, astonished, made her a cup of tea.
"Tea's no answer," said Alison.
"Tea never was an answer," said Mum, "but it was always something to do with your hands, while you got your act together."
A Libation of Blood – FAY WELDON
(*Novelist*)

Bread and water can so easily be toast and tea.
AUTHOR UNKNOWN

✎

American-style iced tea is the perfect drink for a hot, sunny day. It's never really caught on in the UK, probably because the last time we had a hot, sunny day was back in 1957.
TOM HOLT (*Novelist*)

✎

In his very amusing book *Three Men in a Boat*, Jerome K. Jerome wrote, "It is very strange, this domination of our intellect by our digestive organs. We cannot work, we cannot think, unless our stomach wills so. It dictates to us our emotions, our passions. After eggs and bacon it says, "Work!" After beefsteak and porter, it says, "Sleep!" After a cup of tea (two spoonfuls for each cup, and don't let it stand for more than three minutes), it says to the brain, "Now rise, and show your strength. Be eloquent, and deep, and tender; see, with a clear eye, into Nature, and into life: spread your white wings of quivering thought, and soar, a god-like spirit, over the whirling world beneath you, up through long lanes of flaming stars to the gates of eternity!"

✎

My biographers said that my parties reminded them of a vicarage tea party, with sex thrown in. I know it does make people happy, but to me it is just like having a cup of tea.
CYNTHIA PAYNE (*Renowned party hostess*)

✎

Is there no Latin word for Tea? Upon my soul, if I had known that, I would have let the vulgar stuff alone.
HILAIRE BELLOC (1870–1953; *writer*)

✎

We arg'ed the thing at breakfast, we arg'ed the thing at tea, And the more we arg'ed the question, the more we didn't agree.
WILL CARLETON (1845–1912; *poet*)

✎

I love this quote from comic genius BILLY CONNOLLY: "Never trust a man who, when left alone in a room with a tea cosy, doesn't try it on."

✎

"Take some more tea", the March Hare said to Alice very earnestly. "I've had nothing yet", Alice replied in an offended tone, "so I can't take more." "You mean you can't take less", said the Hatter: "it's very easy to take more than nothing."
Alice In Wonderland LEWIS CARROLL (1832–1898; *author*)

Why do they always put mud into coffee on board steamers? Why does the tea generally taste of boiled boots?
The Kickleburys on the Line
WILLIAM MAKEPEACE THACKERAY
(1811–1863; *novelist*)

TEA AND WISDOM

The professional must learn to be moved and touched emotionally, yet at the same time stand back objectively: I've seen a lot of damage done by tea and sympathy.
ANTHONY STORR, quoted in ***The Times***
(1920–2001; *psychiatrist and author*)

It ought to be illegal for an artist to marry. If the artist must marry, let him find someone more interested in art, or his art, or the artist part of him, than in him. After which let them take tea together three times a week.
EZRA POUND (1885–1972; *poet*)

Tea is instant wisdom – just add water!
ASTRID ALAUDA

Architecture is basically a container of something. I hope they will enjoy not so much the teacup, but the tea.
YOSHIO TANIGUCHI (*Architect*)

When we learn to drive a golf ball or play tennis or billiards, when we learn to tell the price of tea by tasting it or to strike a certain note exactly with the voice, we do not learn in the main by virtue of any ideas that are explained to us, by any inferences that we reason out.
EDWARD THORNDIKE
(1874–1949; *psychologist*)

All true tea lovers not only like their tea strong, but like it a little stronger with each year that passes.
A Nice Cup of Tea GEORGE ORWELL
(1903–1950; *author and journalist*)

NB – these following quotes have nothing whatsoever to do with tea, but I had to include them and share them with you, as they're some of my most favourite quotes. How I wish I had come across the wisdom they convey long ago!

Don't be afraid to fail. Don't waste energy trying to cover up failure. Learn from your failures and go on to the next challenge. It is OK to fail. If you are not failing, you are not growing.
H. STANLEY JUDD

We learn from failure much more than from success; we often discover what we will do by finding out what we will not do; and probably he who never made a mistake never made a discovery.
SAMUEL SMILES

Fear is the opportunity for courage, not proof of cowardice.
JOHN MCCAIN

An error doesn't become a mistake until you refuse to correct it.
ORLANDO A. BATTISTA

There can be no real freedom without the freedom to fail.
ERICH FROMM

Failure is only opportunity to more intelligently begin again.
HENRY FORD

Best men are often moulded out of faults.
SHAKESPEARE

Anyone who has never made a mistake has never tried anything new.
ALBERT EINSTEIN

If people did not sometimes do silly things, nothing intelligent would ever get done.
WITTGENSTEIN

If you are not big enough to lose, you are not big enough to win.
WALTER REUTHER

A man should never be ashamed to own he has been wrong, which is but saying in other words that he is wiser today than he was yesterday.
ALEXANDER POPE

So many different and wise ways of saying the same thing! You may well be wondering why I didn't select just one. Well – my feeling is that it is all a matter of personal taste and one of them will speak more directly to you – so I'd rather you make your own choice.

Here are a few more wise sayings that I can't resist sharing with you.

Great works are performed not by strength, but perseverance.
SAMUEL JOHNSON
☙

The quality of a person's life is in direct proportion to their commitment to excellence, regardless of their chosen field of endeavor.
VINCE LOMBARD
☙

I have learnt silence from the talkative, toleration from the intolerant, and kindness from the unkind; yet strange, I am ungrateful to these.
KAHLIL GIBRAN
☙

Reflect upon your present blessings, of which every man has plenty; not on your past misfortunes, of which all men have some.
CHARLES DICKENS
☙

A great attitude does much more than turn on the lights in our worlds; it seems to magically connect us to all sorts of serendipitous opportunities that were somehow absent before we changed.
EARL NIGHTINGALE
☙

"Feeling gratitude and not expressing it is like wrapping a present and not giving it."
WILLIAM AUTHOR WARD –
Author and editor
☙

"When you forgive, you in no way change the past – but you sure do change the future."
BERNARD MELTZER –
lawyer and professor
☙

"Shared joy is a double joy; shared sorrow is half sorrow."
SWEDISH PROVERB
☙

"Nothing is particularly hard if you divide it into small jobs."
HENRY FORD –
Industrialist
☙

"If you have knowledge, let others light their candles in it."
MARGARET FULLER –
Author and teacher
☙

"Freedom of choice requires the realisation that we have a choice."
G. ORME
☙

"Once you replace negative thoughts with positive ones, you'll start having positive results."
WILLIE NELSON – *Singer and Songwriter*
☙

"Time spent laughing is time spent with the Gods."
JAPANESE PROVERB
☙

CHAPTER 11
Fascinating Facts and Trivia

I N THE PROCESS OF DOING RESEARCH FOR THIS BOOK I uncovered all sorts of interesting little tea-related facts and largely useless but amusing anecdotes that I would like to share with you. So, here they are in no particular order.

Tea Caddies

Because tea was so expensive when it first arrived in England, it was kept in locked wooden boxes – tea caddies. The word "caddy" comes from the Asian word catty – a unit of weight applied to tea – usually about 600 grams (1¼ pounds). These boxes were made of varying types of veneered wood, ivory and even scrolled paper and are now highly prized and valuable items in the world of antiques.

Emperor Hui Tsung and the Virgin Pluckers

Legend has it that Chinese Emperor Hui Tsung (1100–1126) preferred his tea plucked by virgins! They had to pluck the tea with gold scissors and dry the leaves on special gold platters. After infusion, the tea was then poured into the emperor's own special cup.

From Where Does Bone China Get its Name?

When you look at delicate bone china, the bones of cows don't immediately spring to mind! However, it is in fact the addition of bone ash (from cattle bones) to porcelain that makes this lovely white, translucent china so strong.

Where Did Porcelain Get its Name?

The word is thought to be derived from porcella, the Italian word for "shells", because of its translucent quality.

Taiwan Tea Facts

Taiwan is famous for its unique tea culture. Tea shops are everywhere in the North region and are typically open 365 days a year. Almost all of the banks in Taiwan serve tea for their customers and most offices have a big pot of tea, serving their employees and visitors. Iced tea is so popular in Taiwan that they are said to have more varieties of iced tea than all other beverages combined.

What Did English People Drink for Breakfast Before Tea Became Popular?

Before tea became universally available, ale was drunk at breakfast! This was because water was not of a very high standard and ale was a safer option. Maybe that's why people used to whistle more in the old days?!

Saying Goodbye With Tea

Apparently at the end of the Qing Dynasty (1644–1911), the way to tell guests that they had outstayed their welcome was to serve them with tea. The famous quote at that time was: "serve guests with tea and say 'goodbye'".

Tea and the French Populace

Tea only remained popular in France for about 50 years, being replaced by a preference for wine, hot chocolate and coffee.

The Popularity of Tea in Britain

More than any other Western people, the British have made tea-drinking an integral part of their national way of life, savouring its unique property of serving both as a social stimulant and as a pacifier in times of stress.

Tea in Scotland

In 1680, the Duchess of York introduced tea to Scotland.

Tea and Temperance

During the First World War there was a strong temperance movement and tea became a popular alternative to alcohol. By 1938 the British were reputed to be drinking well over 9 pounds of tea, per head per year.

Tea – A Luxury for the Wealthy

When tea first came to Europe it was a luxury only the wealthy could afford. Slowly, as the amount of tea imported increased, the price fell and sales increased.

- In 1662 tea was so rare a commodity in England, that the English East India Company bought 2 pounds 2 ounces of it, as a present for King Charles II.

- In 1666 tea was sold in London for 60 shillings per pound.

- During Queen Anne's reign (1702–1714), British people consumed some 66,000 pounds of tea each year, a figure that had risen to nearly 30,000,000 pounds by 1837, the year in which Queen Victoria ascended the throne.

- A number of famous retailers got their start in the tea business. In 1824 John Cadbury opened a tea and coffee shop in Birmingham, England, which grew into the Cadbury Chocolate Co.

- In 1849, London tea wholesaler Henry Charles Harrod took over a shop that would soon bear his name and become one of the world's most famous department stores.

Taxation and Tea

At its highest, tea tax in England reached 119 per cent and this led to widespread smuggling, which was highly organised. The tea was often stored in churches, and syndicates helped move the smuggled tea around the country. It all came to an end in 1784 when the prime minister, William Pitt (the Younger), passed an act that dramatically cut the tax to 12.5 per cent.

Tea was a Forbidden Pleasure for the Young Queen Victoria

Before she became queen, the young Princess Victoria was not allowed by her governess to drink tea. Apparently, her first words after hearing of her accession at the age of 18 in 1837, were, "Bring me a

Harrods, one of the world's most famous department stores.

cup of tea and *The Times*".

Queen Mary Loved Her Tea

Another royal champion of afternoon tea was Queen Mary, wife of George V (king from 1910–1936) and mother of King Edward VIII, who famously abdicated the throne to marry Wallace Simpson. "Everything had to be fully ready at 4pm punctually," wrote her private secretary, Charles Oliver, "with sandwiches, cakes and biscuits invitingly set out on gleaming silver dishes upon a smoothly running trolley. The teapot, cream jug, hot water jug and sugar bowls were always the same antique silver service, which had been a favourite of Queen Victoria!"

The Duke of Wellington

The Duke of Wellington (1769–1852), legendary national hero, best known for his victory at the Battle of Waterloo, was so devoted to tea that he was always accompanied into battle by his favourite silver tea service.

Twinings Tea Goes Back a Long Way

Thomas Twining converted his coffee shop into The Golden Lyon tea shop, in 1717. It was one of the first shops into which ladies could go unaccompanied to buy their tea. Prior to this, ladies had to send their husbands or male servants into coffee houses, where ladies were forbidden to enter, to purchase the tea for home consumption.

Tea in the Jungle

Intrepid British explorers rarely journeyed through darkest Africa without the where-withal for a "brew-up" in the jungle.

Storing Tea in a Hot-water Bottle

Each night on going to bed, the Victorian prime minister, William Ewart Gladstone, took with him a hot-water bottle filled with boiling hot Assam tea to drink from, should the need arise.

- Next to water, tea is the most commonly consumed beverage in the world.

- Brewed tea leaves mixed with soil make an excellent fertilizer for plants.

TEA – QUICK FACTS

Origins of a Famous Tea Saying

"Not for all the tea in China" is a shortened phrase, first used in Australia in the 1890s which meant, "not at any price".

Tipping

Tipping, as a response to prompt service, started in the tea gardens of England. Small, locked wooden boxes were placed on the tables inscribed with "T.I.P.S.", which stood for "To Insure Prompt Service". If a guest wanted the waiter to hurry, thus ensuring the tea was served hot, he would drop a coin into the T.I.P.S. box.

Adding Milk to Tea

A French woman, Marie de Rabutin-Chantal, the Marquise de Sévigné, made the first mention of adding milk to tea in 1680.

George Orwell's *Essay on Tea*

George Orwell's 1946 essay "A Nice Cup of Tea" laid down 11 steps to the perfect brew, and was a reaction to a lack of guidance on tea brewing in cookbooks.

"This is curious," he wrote in London's *Evening Standard*, "not only because tea is one of the mainstays of civilization in this country… but because the best manner of making it is the subject of violent disputes."

Orwell said tea should be drunk strong, without sugar and from a cup with a round bottom. The tea should be poured before adding milk he insisted, entering a debate that has caused acute controversy within the tea world.

TEA INVENTIONS IN THE USA

The United States can claim two distinct contributions when it comes to tea, both dating from the early twentieth century. They are tea bags and iced tea.

The Tea Bag – An Accidental Invention

It is thought that the tea bag was accidentally invented in 1908 by an American tea importer called Thomas Sullivan. He sent small samples of his tea to potential new customers and packed them in tiny silk bags. They misunderstood and put the entire bags into the pot, thinking that was what he had intended! When future orders did not arrive in the tiny pouches, many people complained and Sullivan, realising the marketing potential, cleverly reacted and went on to invent the first tea bag.

When the bags were commercially produced in America in the 1920s they were initially made of gauze and later this was changed to paper. However, they did not become popular in the United Kingdom until the 1960s. Now 96 per cent of the tea consumed in the UK is brewed using a tea bag.

Traditionally, tea bags have been square or rectangular in shape. More recently circular and pyramidal bags have come on to the market, and are often claimed by the manufacturers to improve the quality of the brew.

Iced Tea

Iced tea was invented during the 1904 World Fair in St Louis, USA. The producers of Indian tea had established a booth to promote their product, but since the weather was uncomfortably hot and humid, nobody bought the steaming drink until the superviser, Richard Blechynden, had the idea to pour it over ice. The rest, as they say, is history. Today, Americans still prefer their tea iced and it accounts for 80 per cent of the tea drunk in the United States.

Iced Tea

SERVES 8

4 regular tea bags of your choice (Assam works well)

2 cups fresh cold water

Ice cubes

Sugar (to taste)

Fresh lemon juice and slices

1. Remove any paper attached to the strings of the tea bags; tie the strings together and place the bags into a large heatproof glass measuring jug.

2. Bring 2 cups cold water (always start with fresh cold water) to a rapid boil and immediately pour over the tea bags. Allow the tea to steep for 20 minutes or more. (This process forms the "concentrate" from which the tea is made).

3. Remove the tea bags from the jug, squeezing out the excess liquid (being careful not to break open the bags) and discard. To serve the iced tea immediately, add a dozen or so ice cubes to the tea concentrate and then fill with enough water to make 4 pints. If you are going to chill the tea and serve later – fill the jug with enough cold water to make 4 pints. Cover and refrigerate until well chilled before serving.

4. To serve, pour the tea over a generous amount of ice cubes in a tall glass, stirring in sugar to taste and a squeeze of lemon, as desired. Add a slice of lemon to each glass.

Adding sugar to iced tea – Americans appear to have strong ideas about whether or not to add sugar to iced tea. It seems to be similar to the English debate about adding milk to tea before or afterwards! I guess, at the end of the day, it's all down to personal preference.

Russian Tea Making

The samovar, which is a Middle Eastern invention, is now most often associated with the culture of Russia and its geographic and cultural neighbours.

The samovar was traditionally a large metal container with a metal pipe running vertically through its centre. To prepare tea, the container was filled with water and charcoal was put in the pipe and lit. When the fire was hot, a teapot would be placed on top of the pipe and a strong concentrate of tea brewed. The tea was served by pouring some of the concentrate into a serving glass, then diluting it with hot water from the main container. Russians traditionally serve their tea in tall, straight-sided glasses, flavoured with lemon or jam. Drinking the tea through a piece of rock sugar held between the teeth was also common.

Apparently modern Russian tea drinkers now use electric samovars, which are available in the West via mail order!

Stats from The United Kingdom Tea Council

The United Kingdom Tea Council (www.tea.co.uk) is an independent non-profit making body dedicated to promoting tea and they regularly publish interesting facts and statistics. Here are some of their latest:

- The British drink 165 million cups per day, which is 60.2 billion per year.

- The number of cups of coffee drunk each day in Britain is estimated at 70 million.

- After the Republic of Ireland, Britain is the largest per capita tea-drinking nation.
- In 2004, China produced 835,000 tonnes of tea, overtaking India who produced 820,000.

- Apart from tourism, tea is the biggest industrial activity in India.

- 96 per cent of British tea is consumed from tea bags.

- 98 per cent of British tea is taken with milk.

- Only 30 per cent of tea drinkers take sugar in their tea.

- 80 per cent of office workers now claim that they find out more about what's going on at work over a cup of tea than in any other way!

SCIENTIFIC TEA MAKING

In 1999 The British Standards Institute recommended that we should "Pour in tea on top of milk to prevent scalding the milk." They also recommend that if you prefer to "... pour your milk in last, the best results are with a liquor temperature of 65–80°C."

The idea of using a thermometer to measure the temperature of your tea is a very sobering thought and not one I would recommend in a million years! Just enjoy your tea the way that YOU like it. See my notes regarding this whole debate on page 28–30.

SUMMARY

I hope you have enjoyed learning the secrets to creating and hosting a delicious afternoon tea. It's certainly been my pleasure guiding you through the process.

One of my greatest joys is hearing of successful teas held by my students and readers. They often email me to let me know how much their friends and family have enjoyed their new-found afternoon tea-making skills! If you do have time, I'd love to hear how you've got on, so please do drop me a line at **giulianaorme@yahoo.co.uk**.

And please don't forget to visit my website at **www.afternoontealessons.com** for updates of my afternoon tea classes etc. and also details of my "Best of British Cooking Classes". These classes offer the opportunity to discover some of Britain's all-time favourite "old fashioned" home-cooked meals and desserts with the occasional modern twist! Once you've tasted these delicious, traditional dishes, you will understand why they are still much loved in British homes today. These fun classes are interactive and after preparation and cooking, we all sit down and have a good "nosh"!

Cheers!